THE BIBLE
AS WORD
OF GOD

TERENCE E. FRETHEIM
KARLFRIED FROEHLICH

THE BIBLE AS WORD OF GOD
In a Postmodern Age

FORTRESS PRESS   Minneapolis

THE BIBLE AS WORD OF GOD
In a Postmodern Age

Library of Congress Cataloging-in-Publication Data

Fretheim, Terence E.
    The Bible as word of God : in a postmodern age / Terence E. Fretheim and Karlfried Froehlich.
        p.   cm.
    Includes bibliographical references.
    ISBN 0-8006-3094-7 (alk. paper)
    1. Bible—Evidences, authority, etc. 2. Bible—Inspiration.
3. Bible—Theology.   I. Froehlich, Karlfried. II. Title.
III. Title: Bible as word of God in a postmodern age.
BS480.F74   1998
220.1'3—dc21   98-40674
                                                                    CIP

Manufactured in the U.S.A.   AF 1-3094

02   01   00   99   98   1   2   3   4   5   6   7   8   9   10

CONTENTS

How is the Bible authoritative in this postmodern age? In this exchange from the 1995 Hein/Fry Lecture Series, Fretheim and Froehlich mount important, though divergent, analyses of the contemporary situation regarding Scripture and suggest varying strategies to meet it.

The Hein/Fry Lectures Committee of the Evangelical Lutheran Church in America set the questions for the two lectures in these terms: What does it mean to say that Scripture has authority for Christian faith and life in light of contemporary forms of biblical criticism? How do we understand a biblical text to be the Word of God when the meaning of the text can vary, depending on the perspective of the reader/hearer? Given the profound hermeneutical challenges of our time, how does Scripture serve as a guide in worship, doctrine, preaching, and ethical decision-making for the people of God?

Church historian Froehlich traces the crisis regarding the Bible to civilizational change and draws on the ecclesial tradition to recover the Word of God as inspired, incarnate, and creative. Old Testament scholar Fretheim, by contrast, wrestles with the reality of postmodernism and the question of how Christians today can deal with problematic aspects of biblical texts, for example, their treatment of women and children. He points to postmodern developments with positive potential for the Bible to speak in our time.

The Hein/Fry Lecture Series is given annually at all eight seminaries of the Evangelical Lutheran Church in America. Commonly, as in 1995, each lecturer speaks at four seminaries. The concern of the series is to engage both the theological leadership of the ELCA and a generation of ministerial candidates in discussion of a focused theological issue.

PART I

By
Karlfried Froehlich

Addressing the topic of these Hein/Fry Lectures is a somewhat scary task for me. What seems to be called for is a decidedly theological treatment, and I am all too aware of my limitations when it comes to constructive theology. I am not a theologian, but a historian—to be precise, a church historian, which is not a very exciting profession in the estimation of many people. Karl Barth called church history an "auxiliary science." That obviously meant that it cannot be regarded as equal to such central fields as exegetical, systematic, and practical theology. At other times I might resent this blatant demotion of my professional calling. On this occasion, however, I am inclined to be grateful for it. Perhaps this classification warns readers not to expect too much of this set of lectures. My lectures do not develop a comprehensive vision of a theology of the Word of God in our time or a proposal of a biblical hermeneutics fit to answer the basic issues debated by concerned theologians of our generation. They will not even provide much of an answer to the very practical questions raised in the announcement of this series. Such answers may have to be supplied by the faith convictions of the readers themselves and by the never-ending dialogue within the church on all levels, from congregational Bible study to the deliberations of our national assemblies. History, however, has its role to play in the discussion of any theological issue. It provides the link to the down-to-earth aspects of all theorizing. It reminds us of the uncomfortable presence of a reality that demands to be taken seriously in all attempts to put things together in a grand synthesis. History is necessary in order to introduce some realistic perspectives into our wrestling with the task of theological construction; even Karl Barth would not have objected to this claim. I hope that some of the perspectives on biblical interpretation I suggest will help all of us to tackle together the formidable task of "rebuilding theological authority" as an important chapter of "A

Common Calling," as the statement of the Lutheran-Reformed Conversations now before the church, has called it.[1]

The topic of these lectures was formulated by the Hein/Fry Committee of the ELCA. Assigned topics, one has to admit, are congenial to a historian. As a historian, I cannot do "my own thing" but have to be open precisely to that which is *not* my own, the unexpected, the different, the constellation I cannot change. Even committees have a place in history. Is there a chance that the Holy Spirit might work through committees? The evidence suggests that there is. There would be no Creed of Nicea, no Chalcedonian Decree, no Formula of Concord without the Holy Spirit *and* a committee. That does not mean, however, that God's providence extends to all and everything a committee says and does. I accepted the assignment of speaking on the topic "The Bible as the Word of God in a Postmodern Age," but the historian in me cringed at the last turn of the phrase: "in a postmodern age." "Postmodern" is a fashionable word these days. It appears frequently in book titles, not only of secular bestsellers but of books on the religion shelves as well. Do those who use it know what they are doing, however? Are they aware of the immense problem created by any periodization of history? For our Western culture it started with the so-called Middle Ages. Why were those eight centuries between 700 and 1500 C.E. called the "middle" ages? What are they in the middle of? Common sense may lead one to the logical answer: The term was created immediately after the Middle Ages ended, and it clearly reflected the self-image of a proud new generation, the people of the Renaissance, who were glad that the old had passed away and everything had become new.[2] Theirs was the *nova aetas,* the "new age," fresh, exciting, and full of promise. *"O Saeculum! What a century!"* exclaimed the young humanist Ulrich von Hutten in the early 1500s. "The humanities are thriving. It is a delight to be alive!" Renaissance means rebirth. That precocious generation was celebrating the cultural rebirth of classical antiquity, the recovery of the highest ideals of humanity at a time of new horizons opening up everywhere—geographically, politically, intellectually, spiritually. It is easy to see why the "Middle Ages" received such a bad name at the hands of the humanists. For them it was the detestable time in the middle, the age of decay, of cultural blight, of linguistic barbarism—in short, the "dark ages" separating the revered antiquity from the light of a new day dawning.

The young generation of Renaissance humanists also spoke of their own time as the "modern" times, *tempora moderna*. "Modern"—this was a fairly new Latin word that had gained currency during the great twelfth century.[3] Derived from the Latin adverb *modo,* "now," it meant "contemporary" or "present." The prefaces of legal deeds very often contained the phrase: "Let all people modern and future know...," meaning those who are alive now as well as those yet unborn. For Shakespeare, "modern" was the equivalent of "common, ordinary": "They say miracles are past; and we have our philosophical persons to make modern and familiar things supernatural and causeless" (*All's Well That Ends Well,* Act III, Scene 2, line 1f.). When the word was used, however, to describe the dominant philosophical party in a late medieval university, it revealed its programmatic potential. The difference between the old way (*via antiqua*) and the "modern" (*via moderna*) affected everything from curriculum and teaching methods to school texts and appointments.[4] This nomenclature reflected a change in the basic value system: What is better—old or new? Earlier centuries valued antiquity; novelty was suspect and was the hallmark of heresy. In the fifteenth and sixteenth centuries, the preferences were changing. The "new" had a stronger attraction; it spelled advance and progress *now.* We have lived in "modern" times ever since. The Great Seal of the United States, designed in 1782 and still printed on every dollar bill, reminds us of this conviction: *Annuit coeptis / Novus ordo seclorum* (The new order of the times—it gives the nod of approval to the things begun). Seen against this background, what then is postmodern? The term may make sense as the designation of an architectural style that arose in reaction to the so-called modern style of the 1920s in the late 1950s, or of a counter-movement against "modernism" among literary critics. But a "postmodern age" as a period of history? I am embarrassed to discover that it was probably a historian, no less a giant than Arnold Toynbee, who introduced it in 1952-53: "Our post-modern Age of Western History."[5] He should have known better.

Or is there perhaps more behind the trendy word-creation? In using the phrase, Toynbee, in a way, was re-ordering Western history. A "postmodern" age implies a "premodern" age, which means that the "modern age " itself has become the new Middle Ages, an age of darkness, danger, and outmoded values. The term in the title of these lectures may well point to a basic shift in the mentality of our age. We are no longer jubilant about the joys of living "now." The "new order" of the American dream has soured on us. The concept of progress meets with suspicion; the "limits of growth" are a troubling concern. We are finished with the optimism of Renaissance and Revolution. "New" is not always better. A mood of *fin-de-siècle* is creeping up on us, a deep sense of the crisis of all values in the institutions that define our lives—the nation, society, the academy, the church. A feeling is in the air that an era is coming to an end, and people are groping for a sense of the new when they are not even sure whether there will be a future, and whether it will be worth living in. What a contrast to the vigorous "modernity" of the early sixteenth century!

The church is not the world, but, living in and for the world, the church cannot help being affected by what is happening around it. The list of questions that accompany the announcement of these lectures leads us deeply into the crisis as it is experienced in our churches: "What does it mean to say that Scripture is authoritative for Christian faith and life in light of contemporary forms of biblical criticism? How do we understand a biblical text to be the Word of God, when the meaning of the text can vary, depending on the perspective of the hearer? Given the profound challenges of our time, how does Scripture serve as a guide in worship, doctrine, preaching, and moral and ethical decision making for the people of God?" These questions aptly describe the crisis as a crisis of authority, specifically the authority of the Bible. The Bible's authority is indeed a neuralgic point, perhaps *the* neuralgic point, for our people and their pastoral leadership in the 1990s. It is where the traditional gap between the church and the academy seems to have widened more than anywhere else. Many thoughtful people in the ELCA are alarmed at the situation. To be sure, crisis is always better than a false peace. It is the point where new hope arises. As Père Lacordaire, one of the great French preachers of the nineteenth century, once remarked, sowing and planting is best done when the sky is overcast and the weather is stormy.[6]

We *must* speak of the Bible when we speak of authority in a Christian church. It has been said that the notion of authority is analytic to Scripture;[7] that is, the term "Scripture" implies an authority claimed or accorded by definition inasmuch as it refers to a specific canon governing faith and action in a community, not to a random collection of writings. Protestants know the compelling need to keep the Bible at the forefront even more forcefully than other Christian church bodies. In espousing the "scriptural principle" of the sixteenth-century Reformation, they drew back from a broader culturally and socially anchored basis of authority and staked everything on one source, and one source only: *Sola Scriptura*. We will have to ask what this phrase has meant and what it can plausibly mean today. Some of us may even want to question whether it was—or is—the right move to make in the arena of authority. Traditionalist Roman Catholic and Eastern Orthodox churches with their broader base of ecclesiastical authority, which includes tradition, pope, and councils, seem to be more in tune with Toynbee's new paradigm; they are less troubled by the disillusionment of a postmodern era because, in the popular mind, they are less identified with modernity and remain tied more closely to the premodern era by their history as well as by choice. What was seen as a weakness not long ago is now perceived as a strength. A number of Lutheran theologians in recent years have judged it their ecumenical duty to convert to Roman Catholicism or Eastern Orthodoxy. But the ecumenical situation seems to me less clear-cut than what the either-or of such steps suggests to the nostalgic and impatient ecumenical instincts of our generation. Even in the early Reformation era, Luther and his friends did attempt to broaden their basis of authority beyond a raw *sola scriptura*. Luther himself appealed to his authority as an academic teacher of the Bible for much of his polemic in the controversy over indulgences: It was his professional duty to say what he said.[8] He and his colleagues did not hesitate to call on the authority of secular rulers to put their biblically based reform ideas into practice. It was the sectarian groups, not the territorial churches of the magisterial Reformers, that attempted to live "by the Bible alone." Subsequent Lutheranism dropped even heavier authority anchors into the societal structures, the cultures, and the ethnic communities in which its adherents participated; its *sola scriptura* functioned in institutional frameworks that qualified the *sola* considerably. Roman Catholics, on the other hand, have become far more aware in recent decades of their own tradition of privileging scriptural authority. The statements of the Lutheran–Roman Catholic Dialogue in this country bear witness to this development.[9] In all of them, the argument from Scripture is not only important but decisive for the convergence claimed. An analysis of the 1985 statement on "Justification by Faith" would reveal that the measure of consensus described there is developed directly from the exegetical section at the center of the document. Two biblical studies were commissioned by the Dialogue: *Peter in the New Testament* (1973) and *Mary in the New Testament* (1978). The methodological introduction to *Peter in the New Testament* is still one of the best statements of an ecumenical consensus in applying common historical-critical methods to biblical texts. When we speak of the authority of the Bible, Lutherans and Roman Catholics sit in the same boat. We face the same problems, and we share the same challenges.[10]

We sit even closer to our Reformed partners in this matter. The recent Lutheran-Reformed Conversations have made it clear that all the churches involved share the constitutional commitment to the authority of Scripture and its normative role for their faith and life.[11] They all are conscious of their common roots in the Reformation principles of the sixteenth century, and their ordination questions reflect the commitment of their candidates for ministry in wording similar to that in *Lutheran Book of Worship*: "The Church in which you are to be ordained confesses that the Holy Scriptures are the Word of God and are the norm of its faith and life." We *must* speak of the Bible when we speak of authority in the churches of the Reformation.

We must also speak of the "Word of God" when we speak of authority in the church. The reason is not only that our constitutional texts do so, and that many of our ancestors used the term "Word of God" practically synonymous with Scripture, but that the *Deus loquens,* the "speaking God," is a foundational experience of both the Christian community of faith and its Jewish matrix. James I. Packer, a prominent member of the "International Council on Biblical Inerrancy," entitled a book propagating the ideas of the 1978 "Chicago Statement on Biblical Inerrancy" *God Has Spoken.*[12] The title shows that he is not a Lutheran. *God Is Speaking* would be the Lutheran version. The reality of God among us is the reality of a living voice, *viva vox,* the proclamation of what God is saying *today* because he has said it *eph' hapax*—once, but precisely once *for all.* Luther would not have known how to separate the scriptural Word of God from the one that is proclaimed and heard in the present, "modern" times. This means first that a church that bears his name is committed not just to be a talking but also a listening church. It means, second, that there is an expectation among us that if we listen we *will* hear God's Word. It is a characteristic tenet of the Lutheran tradition that this hearing, both individual and communal, is not an unmediated internal phenomenon but has a prior, external dimension: The inner word (*verbum internum*) is preceded and mediated by the outer word (*verbum externum*), Scripture and its proclamation. Scripture is the mean. Here it is again, the problem of the middle term and its precarious role in the shifting tides of any contemporary consciousness. The questions formulated by the Hein/Fry Committee express the depth of the anguish: How *can* we hear God's Word today when it does not reach us directly but is mediated through this embarrassing book? Naturally, the problem seems to lie with the middle term: We are all aware that there are real problems with the Scriptures. Could it be that there is also a problem with the two poles on either side—with God who seems to us more hidden than revealed in the book, and with us, who have a hard time listening to anyone, let alone the Bible? Thomas Aquinas could call sin an "impediment" (*obex*), a "roadblock," which humans throw in the way toward the goal of their own lives. Perhaps by taking seriously this analysis of our situation while keeping the possibility of the *Deus loquens,* God wanting to speak to us out of his hiddenness, as a point of departure for our deliberations, we can gain some perspectives on the problems that bother us.

The following remarks are organized under three headings, (1) The Inspired Word of God: Authority and Inspiration; (2) The Incarnate Word of God: Experience and Language; (3) The Creative Word of God: Tradition and Interpretation. For each section, I have added a scriptural motto, a "protheme" as it was called in medieval sermons and disputations, which may serve as a brief summary of the argument.

CHAPTER 1

The Inspired Word of God: Authority and Inspiration

"God does not lie." *(Titus 1:2)*

T HE CRISIS OF BIBLICAL AUTHORITY IN OUR CHURCHES MUST BE SEEN IN THE wider context of the general crisis of authority in today's culture—a culture from which the notion of the Bible as an authoritative word for everyone has long since vanished. Jeffrey Stout, a philosopher and ethicist at Princeton University, published a thoughtful study on this crisis in 1981. He titled it *The Flight from Authority: Religion, Morality, and the Quest for Autonomy.*[13] I have some admiration for an engaged thinker who says he is not a Christian, not even a "religionist," but who wants to explore the chances of a unified rational discourse in a world of centrifugal dynamics. It seems like the task of squaring the circle. But Stout is a fine historian; if nothing else, his analyses of the great intellectual shifts in the last two hundred years are worth reading. The title reveals the thesis: With the demise of central decision-making in politics and religion during the two centuries following the Reformation, the flight from authority was an accomplished fact. The alternative, a Cartesian reliance on self-evident rational truth or its scientifically derived approximations, however, has proved to be equally elusive. Stout concludes that no "foundationalism" will work any more in the future. What is needed is a "holistic" approach to moral discourse that must proceed pragmatically and must be geared toward consensus both vertically (among inherited ethical traditions) and horizontally (among different cultures). Of course, much has happened since 1981. If Stout still assumed that, from the standpoint of philosophy, morality was safe but theism was in trouble, one is tempted to argue the contrary today: religion is flourishing again, certainly in its sectarian forms, but morality is in big trouble. Indeed, the flight from authority appears to be complete. There are no universal, unquestioned authority structures any more. And the alternative, autonomous reason? Stout is certainly correct when he points to the deep crisis here, too. One wonders whether, in the self-centered culture of the late 1990s, reason has not been replaced already by sheer opportunism, irrational or pseudo-rational prejudice, and personal choice.

There can be hardly any doubt that the present crisis of biblical authority is linked to the phases of Western intellectual history outlined by Stout. In the wake of the "flight from authority," Protestantism's elevated norm of Scripture was destined for even more trouble when the alternative option of autonomous reason was beginning to be practiced on it. Maurice Wiles, former Dean of Christ Church, Oxford, and a noted church historian, observes that the main strategy in the churches has been to develop and refine the methods of critical Bible study rather than face the real problem: "It may be that we would do better to look for a modification of the role expected of Scripture in the Church than to search for a more congenial style of criticism."[14] Wiles finds himself in the company of other British scholars, such as James Barr, John Hick, and John Barton, when he suggests that we should learn "to see scripture as an indispensable *resource* rather than as binding authority."[15] This point is made by an increasing number of scholars on this side of the Atlantic as well. One of the most outspoken is Robin Scroggs of Union Seminary in New York. Scroggs answers his own question, "Does the claim that the Bible has authority any longer make sense?" in a twofold way. Negatively, "I propose . . . that we forthrightly give up any claim that the Bible is authoritative (as I have defined the word) in guidance for contemporary faith and morals." Positively, "What we need . . . is an understanding that takes the Bible as foundational document but not as authoritative, that is, an understanding that does not assume that the Bible determines all that we are to think and do."[16] In reaction to Wiles, I have always resented being listed as a "resource" in the promotional literature of Princeton institutions to be deployed, so to speak, at their beck and call rather than by my own choice, and I am sure the Bible does not like this label either. Scrogg's reduction of the Bible to the status of a "foundational document of Christianity" and as such "absolutely indispensable in learning what it means to be a Christian," on the other hand, strikes me as a self-serving argument within the narrow circle of an academic guild that is clear about its scientific principles but oblivious of the communities to which it is speaking, except its own. It is as if a German theologian were eagerly seeking to converse with Jews because "knowledge of the Jewish background is absolutely indispensable for our Christian self-understanding." True enough, but such a person would want to talk to members of a community where his self-centered presumption could only add insult to injury.

The above quotations also raise the question of the nature of authority itself, which we have left out so far. Stout refuses to give any definition. Scroggs at one point speaks of authority as a "legal" phenomenon. Historically, he is on the right track with this observation. The Latin term *auctoritas,* which is at the root of the English word, designated the legal power of issuing commands and orders to be obeyed in imperial Rome, a power that the emperor and his administration possessed.[17] It included the power of enforcement through legal sanctions. The idea of law is a dynamic process that includes three steps: promulgation, crisis, enforcement. It is the third element that finally determines the nature of law as law. Law that cannot be enforced is not yet actual law. Law that has not been enforced has ceased to be law. Early Christian thinking about law in the life of the community replaced the third element by the reference to the eschatological judgment. Thus it created an unusual concept—eschatological law.[18] Despite all claims to the contrary, the legal authority of bishops and popes never enjoyed the same political and social power as that of secular rulers because it lacked enforcement. Excommunication as a sanction avoided the problem by simply placing offenders in a different social context, locating them outside the protection of the law—not a comfortable situation, of course, in a Christianized empire! "Authority" in the context of the Christian church thus came closer to the pre-imperial use of the term where *auctoritas* was distinguished as "counsel" or "advice" from *potestas* as enforceable legal power. The Roman senate under the Republic had *auctoritas,* the right of deliberation and advisement, but not *potestas* or *imperium,* the power of coercion. If we were to analyze the more comprehensive notion of authority in contemporary understanding, power would be one of two poles, acceptance or recognition the other, with reason or legitimation serving as the middle term. In the various domains of public life, the accents will be placed differently: in the political realm, power establishes authority, and since it can force compliance, it acts as coercive authority. In the realm of science, rational investigation establishes authority, an authority that is universally accepted and exercises power. In the religious realm, acceptance alone establishes authority, an authority that is unable to motivate compliance except by persuasion. The dynamics of the process point to the *relational* character of authority: Like law, authority does not exist in the abstract. It is the result of the interplay of several factors. It must be claimed or exercised, then weighed or validated, and finally enforced or accepted. Among the many definitions of authority that may be helpful in our context, I am particularly impressed by a strongly relational one proposed by the Catholic theologian Avery Dulles: "Authority is that which (or the person whom) one has reason to trust."[19] This definition does not refer to power; in mentioning reason, it refers to warrant, weighing, and legitimation, and it describes the element of acceptance as "trust."

The last point here is probably the most important one: authority has to do with trust. I extend trust, and with this act I bestow power. This is why authority is so vulnerable and so often eyed with suspicion. Trust can be easily misplaced, and the power it gives can be abused in an authoritarian way: oppression, violence, exploitation are the consequences. Understanding authority as trust also highlights its universal necessity for human existence. From earliest childhood on, we must trust those who are close to us. Within the bounds of human community, there is something like a natural parental authority. We also can point to the fact that the phenomenon of authority as interpersonal trust accords fully with the history of the word. *Auctoritas* is derived from the Latin word *auctor*—the author, originator, founder, augmenter of some entity, primarily an ancestor. In ancient Rome, the "authority" of an *ancestor* was not a matter of rights and entitlements passed on to subsequent generations, but a personal influence felt, a task left to be completed by the descendants.

It is tempting to apply this personalist concept to biblical authority. Since the Enlightenment, the attention of exegetes has shifted to the human authors of biblical books. Even Scroggs grants them the authority of furnishing the indispensable material for our understanding of the foundations of Christian identity. They left a personal influence, and this "authority" has led to an intensive acquaintance with their person. Modern historical exegesis has brought the biblical authors, even those whose names we do not know, quite close to us across the "wide, ugly ditch" of history that separates them from us.[20] Engaged exegetes know their Jeremiah, their Luke, Paul, or James as if these authors were the people in the pictures of the family album. They can paint a vivid portrait of the personality, explain the thoughts and intentions of these ancestors, chat with them as with colleagues, and pat them on the back. We all have shared in and profited from this conviviality when we have considered biblical texts. It is a remarkable achievement that has opened up the joy of Bible study to countless people in our pews and adult education groups. But the commitment of the church community in which we read the Bible still goes beyond this level of jovial familiarity. "This church accepts the canonical Scriptures of the Old and New Testaments as the inspired Word of God"—not only as Word of God, which should be scary enough if we take God seriously, but as "the *inspired* Word of God." Here it is, that dread word "inspired," from which many Lutherans draw back as soon as they hear it.

Most of us who love the playground of down-to-earth exegesis are probably uneasy when we have to think of "inspired" Scripture. It is as if the face of the parent suddenly appears at the fence—the threat of authority, ready to lift the finger and to say, "Playtime is over. Let's go home." The Christian notion of biblical inspiration suggests indeed that, in one sense or another, God is the *auctor* of Scripture. "God, the author of Holy Scripture" (*Deus auctor sacrae scripturae*) is an old Latin formula that appears in conciliar documents from the fourth century on.[21] It was probably coined against the Manichean rejection of the Old Testament, insisting that the same God stands behind both Testaments, the God of Abraham, Isaac, and Jacob as well as the God of Jesus and Paul. The suggestion is not that God must be claimed as a *literary* author, a writer. *Auctor,* as we just saw, means first of all originator, founder, beginner. This broader understanding has allowed theologians over the centuries to define the relation between the initiative of God and the human authorship of the biblical books in other than mechanistic terms. According to them, God is the primary author, the biblical writers the secondary authors. Or, as the scholastic theologians of the thirteenth century formulated in the terms of Aristotelian causation: God is the efficient, the human writers the instrumental cause of the books.[22] Many Christians feel comfortable with this explanation. Do we need more? Why a doctrine of inspiration?

The doctrine of biblical inspiration is deeply embedded in the tradition of our Lutheran churches from the time of Lutheran orthodoxy, and Lutherans are not the only ones who carry its burden. When I was appointed to the Benjamin B. Warfield chair at Princeton Seminary, I had not read much of Warfield's publications. It was too late to follow the example of a colleague from another institution who had been offered the Charles Hodge professorship at Princeton but declined politely after he had read some of Hodge's writings. Hodge and Warfield were the staunch advocates of a Presbyterian orthodoxy that applied all the intellectual powers at its disposal to the explication and defense of this very doctrine.

"Inspired"—the word is biblical, but it occurs only once in the canon, at 2 Tim 3:16: "All scripture is inspired by God (*theo-pneustos*) and profitable for teaching, for reproof, for correction, and for training in righteousness."[23] It speaks of God, Spirit, and Scripture in combination, evoking the memory of "God-breathing" connected with the creation of Adam (Gen 2:7). The idea of divine writings was not unknown in antiquity. It occurred in two forms: divinely written *texts* and divinely inspired *writers*. In ancient Israel, it was possible to say that Yahweh "wrote" the tablets of the covenant: "The tablets were the work of God, and the writing was the writing of God, graven upon the tablets" (Exod 32:16; cf. 24:12; 31:18), or at least that God dictated them (Exod 34:27-28; cf. *Jub* 1–2). This, however, is quite different from the Greek notion of inspiration. The latter is closer to the phenomenon of prophecy in the Hebrew Scriptures; Israel's prophets "received" the Word of God and then proclaimed it orally and in written form. Greek inspiration stressed the ecstatic element: The deity communicated through persons whom it had "seized," "filled," "enthused." Inspired writers, the poets of old, wrote in "ecstasy," in a state of being "out of their mind," blissfully unaware of what they were saying. This was the very reason why Plato, while admiring their art, did not want to assign to them the task of educators in his ideal *politeia*.[24] Both concepts, the inspiration of texts and of people as instruments of divine communication, were combined in the Greek-speaking Jewish community. For Philo of Alexandria, all the writers of biblical books were "prophets" who received their messages directly from God in an ecstatic experience, a divine frenzy, in which, deprived of mental activity of their own, they became "the vocal instrument of God, plucked and played by his invisible hand."[25] Moses was the prime example.

Philo, however, could also present holy *texts* as being inspired. This becomes clear in his reception of the Septuagint legend, the story of the origin of the famous Greek translation of the Hebrew Scriptures.[26] The earlier form, which is told in the *Letter of Aristeas* (ca. 170 B.C.E.), speaks of a group of seventy-two translators who, at the invitation of a Ptolemaic king in Egypt, translated the Hebrew Scriptures in seventy-two days and submitted their work to the Jewish community at Alexandria for approval before presenting it to the king. In Philo, the tale is somewhat different: "Sitting on the island in seclusion with none present save the elements of nature—earth, water, air, heaven . . . they became as it were possessed, and under inspiration wrote, not each several scribe something different but the same word for word, as though dictated to each by an invisible prompter."[27] Christians embellished the story further. By the end of the fourth century, Epiphanius tells of the seventy-two elders working in pairs on the entire Bible in thirty-six separate cells. When all the translations were compared, they turned out to be identical. Augustine was so impressed by this massive inspiration that he told his correspondent, Jerome, that he would much prefer to see an authoritative Latin translation from the Septuagint produced by the great scholar of Bethlehem rather than a translation from the original Hebrew.[28]

Today, the doctrine of biblical inspiration is the basis of authority in many fundamentalist and evangelical churches in this country and elsewhere. "To speak of Scripture's authority is to make a statement about God who inspired it."[29] In the more conservative circles, the watchword nowadays is "inerrancy." Like "infallibility," "inerrancy" is an indication of a defensive posture. A person who opts for biblical "inerrancy" wants to exclude any possible error; someone who advocates "infallibility" wants to rule out any thought of fallibility. A similar defensive posture can be detected behind the stress on the doctrine of inspiration in Lutheran and Reformed orthodoxy.[30] Neither the Augsburg Confession nor the Formula of Concord included a systematic article on Scripture, and even Martin Chemnitz's *Examination of the Council of Trent* did not discuss inspiration separately as a topic or article of controversial theology. Lutheran polemicists of the seventeenth century blamed the need to develop the article on the Jesuits who, they suggested, were casting doubts on the shared doctrine in order to establish the necessity of unwritten traditions. The accent here fell on sufficiency, not on inerrancy. Another adversary emerged with the Socinians who, while recognizing the authority of the Bible, doubted its reliability at many points. When the doctrine was firmly in place, the representatives of the new rational sciences had already begun to voice doubts about historical details. Reasons enough to be on the defense. But where exactly is the threat? What must be defended?

Infallibilists and inerrantists maintain that nothing less than God's own veracity is at stake. Indeed, the syllogism seems compelling: God is Truth. The Bible is the Word of God. Therefore, the Bible must be true or God is made a liar. "God cannot lie"—this is the battle cry of the Council on Inerrancy. The phrase itself is the King James translation of Titus 1:2 (*apseudes theos*), and its substance occurs in several places in the Bible, including Num 23:19, where the contrast is noted: "God is not a *human being* that he should lie." The latter point is emphasized in Psalm 116:11 ("I said in my consternation: Everyone is a liar"), which Paul quotes in Rom 3:4: "Although everyone is a liar, let God be proved true." The Vulgate formulates the sentence as a pun: *Deus verax, omnis autem homo mendax.*[31] Lying here includes the will to deceive, an intra-mental psychological phenomenon to which Augustine devoted two entire treatises.[32] What is at issue, however, cannot be God's moral character. God, who is the Truth, needs no defense. The trouble with almost all modern theories of inspiration and inerrancy is that they do not defend the veracity of God or even the veracity of the Bible but only one small part of the whole picture of God and the Bible, the truth of the *literal sense of Scripture,* the only one of the traditional four senses that remained in place after the Reformation. In the medieval tradition, the "literal" sense (*littera*) still was synonymous with the "historical" (*historia*), even though the meaning of "history" differed vastly from the modern notion and came much closer to "story" or "narrative of events."[33] Most modern doctrines of inspiration are defensive reactions to the erosion of trust in the *literal* veracity of the historical narrative in the court of scientific historical research.

The protection of the literal sense of Scripture was certainly not the intention of the doctrine of inspiration in early Christian centuries. On the contrary. Take Origen of Alexandria. Origen had a very high opinion of biblical inspiration.[34] The notion included not only the inspiration of the writers but of every word, every turn of the phrase, every error of a scribe, indeed, of the entire history of the transmission of the text. It was all in God's plan. And Origen drew far-reaching conclusions: If the Scriptures are *in-spired,* if God the Spirit speaks through them, they must be read "spiritually." Although every passage in the Bible has a spiritual sense, many do not also have a literal sense. Origen was not afraid of finding errors, impossibilities, contradictions, and even fictitious historical events on the literal level. He sought them out with care; he exposed them with glee, for he was convinced that their presence had a purpose. Such stumbling blocks pointed unmistakably to the need of a deeper understanding.

> "To be specific: What intelligent person can believe that there was a first day, then a second and third day, evening, and morning, without the sun, the moon, and the stars; and the first day—if this is the right term—even without a heaven? Who is foolish enough to believe that, like a human farmer, God planted a garden to the East of Eden and created in it a visible, physical tree of life from which anyone tasting its fruit with bodily teeth would receive life. . .? When God is depicted walking in the garden in the evening and Adam hiding behind the tree, I think no one will doubt that these details point figuratively so some mysteries by means of a historical narrative which seems to have happened but did not happen in a bodily sense."[35]

Reading God's inspired Scriptures was the dynamic process of a spiritual ascent (*anagoge*) from the letter to higher "mysteries." This process of spiritual reading freed the texts from the fetters of a narrow literalism and from their timebound limitations. It allowed Christians to read the Old and New Testament *together* as the Word of the same God and to explore the true mystery of human existence—the journey of the soul to God.

Origen's anagogical hermeneutics became the basis for the theory of a fourfold sense in the Middle Ages in which the "spiritual" sense was subdivided into allegory, tropology, and anagogy.[36] Augustine had already added the thought that, in providing guidance for our Godward journey, not only the words of the Bible, but also the things they designate have more than one meaning; in the last analysis, they all speak of God as the beginning and the end of everything.[37] How does one find this meaning? Augustine recommended hard work on the text, using every technical tool at one's disposal, from the study of Greek to the basic knowledge of the liberal arts, then prayer and more Bible study. The medieval monastic communities developed the way of "divine reading" (*lectio divina*), reading aloud and rereading the biblical texts, memorizing and contemplating them in solitude as well as in a communal context. And finally, there were tools for Bible study. The *Glossa ordinaria,* that standard biblical commentary of the High Middle Ages, while also giving word explanations, was primarily a compend of spiritual commentary on all the books of the Bible, culled from the patristic exegetical literature. It was in this form that the Bible was read and taught in pastor's studies, schools, and universities. Anagogical hermeneutics explain why medieval readers were aware of variant readings in their biblical text but were not much bothered by them. Anagogical hermeneutics also explains why medieval theologians could extend the reach of divine inspiration quite considerably. Hugh of St. Victor in the twelfth century repeated the story of the inspired Septuagint, noting the doubts of Saint Jerome. When he described the perimeters of Holy Scripture, he did not mention inspiration expressly, but his list of the presumably inspired "books of the New Testament" is amazingly wide-ranging. It comprises "the Gospel, the Apostles, *and the Fathers.*"[38] Such a bold expansion had its dangers, of course. The Reformers protested that in Roman Catholicism "tradition" was being accorded the same authority as Scripture; they called the church back to its roots: *Sola Scriptura.* The point is that the doctrine of inspiration does not need to end up as a defensive weapon in a desperate battle with modern science. The notion of an inspired Bible can free the texts from the strictures of their original historical settings, as important as these are for a critical appreciation, and open them up for a new contextualization. It can allow them to blossom afresh and to lead us into new dimensions of our journey.

Feminist theologians have for quite some time argued for such a new contextualization that would not only allow for the revision of prejudice and bias in the texts themselves and their traditional interpretation but would also lead to new forms of community. For Elisa-beth Schüssler Fiorenza, one of the most provocative and imaginative women interpreters of our generation, the hermeneutical center of feminist interpretation has shifted to women-church, "the movement of self-identified women and women-identified men in biblical reli-gion."[39] In her discussion of authoritative religious literature, she makes a distinction between archetype and prototype. Ascribing to a text an archetypal authority means to regard it as an unchanging, timeless pattern from which norms must be culled. A text that is seen as prototype is a beginning, a first historical embodiment of a content that is open to its own transformation. Indeed, it is waiting to be transformed, to be lived out in a new mode of liberated existence. I cannot but agree. I may not count myself as a member of women-church, but this expectant approach to the texts may well be the direction in which our thinking on biblical authority under the inspiring guidance of the Spirit should move in the *oikumene*, the whole church of Christ.

CHAPTER 2

The Incarnate Word of God: Experience and Language

"The word became flesh." (John 1:14)

W E SPOKE OF A LIBERATING DOCTRINE OF INSPIRATION, A DOCTRINE THAT has the power to free the ancient texts from their timebound fetters. We noted already that the very notion of authoritative "Scriptures" implies a "canon." When the ELCA constitution speaks of its commitment to the inspired Word of God, it names as its object "the canonical Scriptures of the Old and New Testaments." The Greek word *kanon* means a measuring rod, rule, or standard. In classical Greek, it was applied to collections of authoritative writings as well as several kinds of lists and tables.[40] Its use as a designation for the collection of Christian biblical books began in the fourth century, at the time when the actual parameter of the collection was being settled by a first round of official actions in the various parts of the Roman Empire.

The Christian biblical canon evolved over a long period of time through a process of selection rather than accretion. This accounts for the variations among earlier canon lists and biblical manuscripts. Some of the early manuscripts of the Greek New Testament (for example, *Codex Alexandrinus; Codex Sinaiticus*) include writings such as the *Epistle of Barnabas,* the *Shepherd of Hermas, First* and *Second Clement,* which apparently were regarded as "authoritative" books in the communities in which they were read. The Alexandrian canon of the Greek Old Testament included more books than the Hebrew canon in use among Jews in Palestine since the end of the first century C.E., which was probably trimmed from a wider pool of writings for polemical reasons. Some scholars have suggested that the more extensive Greek canon would form a more appropriate basis for the concept of canonical Scriptures among Protestants as it does for Roman Catholics, since it retains the witnesses to the apocalyptic strand of the Jewish tradition eliminated by the Pharisaic recension. Moreover, the canonicity of some books was in dispute among Christians for a long time. Jerome notes that the Epistle to the Hebrews was accepted everywhere in the East at his time, but not in the West. The East, on the other hand, did not generally accept the book of Revelation; to this day it is not included in the official lectionary of the Greek church. Initially highly esteemed and widely read, the Apocalypse seems to have suffered a serious setback in the Eastern churches in the century after Origen. Without taking sides, the fourth-century historian Eusebius quotes a long text from Dionysius of Alexandria, who, on the grounds of stylistic differences and other indications, argued that the book was not written by the author of the Gospel, the Apostle John.[41] This quotation shows that, at least in the eyes of Dionysius and Eusebius, one criterion of selection was a historical assumption: only apostolic writings should be accepted into a Christian New Testament. We know today that neither these two writers nor their colleagues had any reliable means of verifying the apostolicity of the writings with which they were dealing. The emerging canon of the New Testament contained quite a few books not written by apostles or their immediate disciples. Obviously, the historical criterion of apostolicity cannot be the only one in making a decision about the acceptance of a particular book as canonical. Furthermore, "one canon" did not guarantee "one text." Bart Ehrmann has shown that variants were inserted for doctrinal reasons and accepted into the copies of canonical books as late as the fourth and fifth centuries.[42] The final list of the Christian canon, authorized and trusted in the church of the later centuries, was an analytic judgment about *coherence* among the books that were selected, a "basic construal" of a coherent entity, to use a phrase of David Kelsey—complex and imaginative, but not arbitrary and inexplicable.[43] Bruce Metzger has said that the church of the early centuries did not "create" the New Testament canon but came to affirm and confirm the self-authenticating quality of certain documents that had proved their worth in its internal and external struggles.[44]

The formation of a biblical canon in the Christian communities, which included the annexation of Jewish Scriptures and the authorization of a number of new writings, had important consequences. It "re-contextualized" each individual book, giving it a place in a new setting in addition to, and different from, its original *Sitz-im-Leben*. This re-contextualization is a major focus of attention for "canonical interpretation" and "canonical criticism," an exegetical method vigorously advocated by Brevard Childs and James Sanders in recent years.[45] It also calls for "intertextual" reading, another methodological innovation that is finding more and more interest today: Individual books or texts are being read with an eye on possible associations and connections with other texts that might naturally occur to ancient or modern readers.[46] The main point to be made about the Christian "canon" is that this concept, like inspiration, needs to be freed from a narrow and defensive understanding. We live with the particular historical selection of past generations, but the canon is only relatively closed. It is conceivable that one of the lost Pauline Epistles or a totally unknown letter of his undoubted authorship will be discovered some day. True, the church would not have a chance to have lived with this book in the past, but only irrelevance would be a valid argument against a decision to receive it into the canon of existing writings and living with it in the future as equally "inspired."

The link between canon and inspiration, which we are touching here, is intriguing. Some years ago, Everett Kalin found that the idea that nonscriptural literature equals noninspired was not true for the early church.[47] "Noninspired" was the epithet of a specific group of writings, those regarded as heretical. Divine "inspiration," on the other hand, could be claimed for a variety of phenomena in the community, including the selection of a canon, of the books that were to have authority. If inspiration does not *establish* authority, but *reflects* an accorded authority, some new perspectives may open up. Consider, for instance, the holy books of other religious traditions: the Quran, or Buddhist and Hindu scriptures. They will certainly not make it into the Christian canon, but could Christians admit some inspiration for them as well? Could we accept the idea that the composition of such writings may have enjoyed some assistance of the Spirit of God?[48] The reason even to ask such a bold question is that Christians think their own inspired Scriptures exist for a purpose. The Scriptures do not have authority, trustworthiness, in the abstract, apart from the divine intention which granted them existence. Their authority is practical rather than absolute, functional rather than ontological.

What are the Scriptures for? In his handbook of biblical hermeneutics, Augustine argues that the central purpose of Scripture is promoting the double love of God and neighbor: "Whoever therefore thinks that he understands the divine Scriptures or any part of them so that it does not build the double love of God and our neighbor, does not understand it at all."[49] There is one intriguing passage in the same treatise, easily overlooked, where Augustine draws out the consequences of this functional view of Scripture: "Thus, a person supported by faith, hope, and charity, with an unshaken hold upon them, does not need the scriptures except for the instruction of others."[50] The statement sounds shocking. There are people who do not need the Bible? Augustine is thinking of the desert saints who "live by these three things [faith, hope, charity] in solitude without books." But even given a degree of admiration for those inspired heroes of the faith, this seems a dangerous conclusion. Is there no limit to inspiration? Can just anything or anyone be called "inspired" when the love of God and neighbor are in evidence? Augustine must have wrestled with questions like these himself. In the *Confessions,* he reports that one of his conversions occurred while he was reading the "books of the Platonists," apparently translations of Neoplatonic writings. He found in them much "Christian" teaching: the upward journey of the soul, the centrality of love, even much of the content of the Johannine Prologue, John 1:1-18. What he did not find was the mediator of the ascent, Jesus Christ, in whom God's love had first come to dwell among us before we could take off.

"I read there that God the Word was born 'not of flesh and blood, nor of the will of man, nor the will of the flesh, but of God.' But that 'the Word was made flesh and dwelt among us,' I found this nowhere there. . . . I read further in them that before all time and beyond all times, thy only Son remains unchangeably coeternal with you, and that of his fulness all souls receive that they may be blessed. . . . But that 'in due time, Christ died for the ungodly' and that you did not spare your only Son but delivered him up for us all—this is not there."[51]

The reality of God's action in the human person of Jesus Christ—this is the point where the expansion of canon and inspiration is stopped, must be reversed and come home. So far, I have not found a use of Augustine's "dangerous" passage in the literature of the Middle Ages. Luther had his own thoughts about the need for Scripture, as we will see later on, probably without reference to Augustine's treatise. An echo, however, may be detected in the writings of Lutheran orthodoxy. In their discussion of the "necessity of Scripture," Lutheran theologians of the seventeenth century distinguished between an "absolute" and a "practical" necessity. There was no absolute necessity for Scripture, they said, but it was given as the means of protecting God's *revelation*.[52]

Here we have another big word in the debate about biblical authority to which we must give attention: revelation. I am personally uneasy at the overpowering presence of this concept in contemporary theological parlance. The term, I think, has been greatly overused and vastly overrated in its usefulness for inner-theological dialogue and apologetics. To be sure, "revelation" is a biblical term. The Latin *revelatio* translates the Greek term *apokalypsis,* the removing of a veil or cover from something that is not seen or is hidden. Both the term and the underlying image play an important role in the Pauline Epistles. The technical use in systematic theology, however, which assumes that there is a body of knowledge given directly by God, is not old.[53] It goes back to the polemics of the sixteenth century and became the focus of attention in the debates over deism in the eighteenth century. Deists claimed that unaided reason can find all necessary religious truth by itself. Christian apologists denied this assertion and pitted revelation against reason. In the nineteenth century, they invoked divine revelation against all kinds of new knowledge connected with the rising tide of the natural sciences. The term took on central significance in the theology of Karl Barth, who recognized its usefulness for his conviction of the absolute priority of God's initiative, *senkrecht von oben,* over any human attempt to get in touch with the divine. Avery Dulles has recently developed a comprehensive typology of contemporary options in theology in a study entitled *Models of Revelation.* The basic understanding of the term here and elsewhere in theology is "the self-disclosure of God"—in nature, in human experience, but preeminently in history—the history of Israel, of Jesus Christ, and of the church.

In a book with the title *Has Christianity a Revelation?* the British philosopher F. Gerald Downing voiced some doubts about the unchecked revelation talk in contemporary theology.[54] The claims made for a Christian revelation are too global, he thought, too high, too total. Arguing from the meaning of the biblical term, he pointed to the inescapably eschatological nature of revelation and warned against rampant theological triumphalism: "Revelation, full personal knowing, may be the final hope and intention. It cannot be the starting point." "There is no knowledge, just faith." The last remark points to the underlying problem. To speak of "revelation" implies privileged knowledge, the license of speaking from God's side, from a vantage point that is not ours to take. I find it instructive that Luther did not use the term in the technical sense. Faith stood in its place for him. "Reason always begins to build on top, at the roof, not below. . . . But God will not have you climb up there this way. He comes to you. He has made a ladder, a path, a bridge to you and says: I will climb down from heaven to you and become human in the Virgin Mary's womb, lie in the manger in Bethlehem, suffer and die for you. Have *faith* in me there. . . . In this *faith,* and with this heart you go upward."[55] With this form of the alternative, Luther followed the tradition: Not *revela-*

tion and reason, but *faith* and reason was the issue. *Faith,* not revelation, is the point from which all knowledge of God arises. There was a specific sense, however, in which "revelation" *was* discussed in Luther's time and before. Following the biblical terminology, a "special" or "personal" revelation from God to individuals was always considered a possibility, even after the death of the last apostle.[56] God did not cease to communicate with humans directly. This conviction was hard won after the Montanist crisis of the late second century, when the visionary authority of new prophets threatened to eclipse the authority of the apostolic churches. It was the affirmation of an ongoing prophetic charism in the church that Augustine, Gregory the Great, and especially Thomas Aquinas kept prominently before the church.[57] Even the medieval code of canon law featured a text that endorsed the "private law" (*lex privata*) of a divine vision as a valid alternative to public church law.[58] It was this affirmation, based as it was on the Pentecostal fulfillment of the scriptural prophecy of Joel: "Your sons *and daughters* shall prophecy" (Joel 2:28 and Acts 2:17), which allowed the voices of at least some women prophets and visionaries to be heard and respected during the Middle Ages as teachers, writers, and theologians in an age of total male domination. To mention only the most obvious cases: Hildegard of Bingen, Mechthild of Magdeburg, Gertrude the Great, and Catherine of Siena. Many more were silenced or never left a trace of their activity and their message. The exercise of a prophetic charism, and even more so the claim to "special revelation," always harbors the potential of disrupting the *status quo* in society and is therefore met by resistance from the powers that be. In the turbulent fifteenth century, not the popular acceptance but the theological authority of this third source of the "knowledge of faith" was waning; claims and partisan interests conflicted too much, and the church's leadership was not strong enough to curb the consequences of these conflicts. Jean Gerson, one of the great theologians of that century, may serve as an illustration of the tragic dilemma.[59] As a French patriot, Gerson defended the visions of Joan of Arc as true revelations of God, but a hostile ecclesiastical court condemned her as a false prophetess and a heretic anyway. He cautioned against the extravagant visions of Bridget of Sweden, but the official church vindicated this visionary and her claims with enthusiasm. In the sixteenth century, Martin Luther rejected the authority of both tradition and special revelation in matters of faith by his insistence on the principle of *sola scriptura*. In the Smalcald Articles of 1537, he even interpreted the pope's presumed teaching authority as a claim to special revelation and held him up for the same scorn as the enthusiasts.[60]

It is in the context of these discussions of "special revelation" that we can hear Luther describing the center of the faith as "revelation" in his own terms: It was the prophets and apostles who received revelations and wrote them down. "Now that the apostles have preached the Word and given their writings, nothing more remains to be revealed than what they have written; no new and special revelation or miracle is needed."[61] What they wrote down, however, was the story of Jesus Christ, a report from faith for faith. "Begin your craft and study with Christ and let it stay and cling there. If your own thoughts and reason or anyone else lead and direct you in a different direction, then close your eyes and say: I am to know and I want to know no other God than in Christ, my Lord."[62] Faith is trust, and trust establishes authority. For Luther, Christ, the Word of God, the Word-Made-Flesh remains the final authority. Luther exemplifies once more the truth that all the necessary expansion of our theological concepts will come to the point where it has to go into reverse: the motion will have to be toward concentration, contraction, and return.

There has to be a return, because in their Christian reading, all these concepts have a definite, "final" anchoring point in history, the history of a particular time, at a particular place, in a particular human person. Yet Jesus is not the person as such but rather the *interpreted* person—a person interpreted by his own history of being born, carrying out a mission, and dying. If we add the incarnation at one end and the resurrection at the other, we have the essence of what Luther called "the gospel," that is, the gospel *story*. Of course, other motions are possible; the Jesus figure can be expanded and projected into a cosmic dimension, as the Epistle to the Ephesians demonstrates and contemporary theologians such as Raimundo Pannikar continue to propose.[63] But all expansion has to submit to the contraction back into history at some point. The motion follows a rhythm, breathing in and breathing out, as it were. In this sense, the Bible in the Christian reading remains totally christocentric *and* at the same time opens up to truly universal dimensions. Attentive readers may have noticed that we are talking here about a controversial concept in Lutheran theology: *Die Mitte der Schrift,* "the center of Scripture," the "canon within the canon."[64] It is often misunderstood. The concept of "canon within the canon" does not refer to a formal criterion, a method of sorting out, prioritizing, and assigning grades to biblical books—central, marginal; important, not important; meat, straw. Like the doctrine of biblical inspiration, it is a hermeneutical device, the description of a necessary movement: You may read any book in the Bible and it will lead you to the center, the gospel. You start from the center—you will find the gospel everywhere.

"Jesus Christ, the incarnate Word," is a rather bold and unusual claim to advance on behalf of a person anchored in history. In fact, this formula of naming the center has a very slim textual basis even in the New Testament. The christological title "Word," *Logos,* is rare indeed.[65] A text such as Heb 1:1-2 does not employ it directly but seems to reflect what it implies: "Long ago, God spoke to our ancestors in many and various ways by the prophets, but in these last days he has spoken to us by a Son." The accent here is on the finality of the anchoring in history. Other forms of "God speaking" are not invalidated, but the emphasis is on God having spoken "in these last days." The author, however, immediately proceeds to expand this center; the cosmic, eternal Son "through whom he also created the worlds," stands at the end of the second of these two verses. This universal dimension is the setting of the Johannine Prologue, where the *Logos* epithet is actually used: Christ is the eternal Word, with the Father from the beginning. The term *logos,* referring to human speech, occurs frequently in John's Gospel, but the majestic title, Jesus Christ as the *Logos* of God, is restricted to those eighteen verses and one faint echo in Rev 19:13.

The textual basis for the "Word *incarnate*" is even slimmer. We do have the two birth stories of the infant Jesus in Matthew and Luke, and Gal 4:4 speaks of God's Son, "born of a woman, born under the law." But the specific notion of the "Word incarnate" emerged from another verse, and one verse only: John 1:14, "the Word became flesh." The Latin translations read: *Verbum caro factum est,* and it was only with the Nicene Creed that the adjective *incarnatus* entered the common theological vocabulary: *Et incarnatus est.* It is amazing to see what can become of just four words when they begin to grow on a community of faith. A neologism, "incarnation" became the dominating paradigm in christology. It served as the focus of Athanasius's soteriological theology: "God was made man that we might be deified."[66] It was exegeted in the Chalcedonian Formula:

> "We all teach harmoniously [that our Lord Jesus Christ is] the same perfect in Godhead, the same perfect in manhood, truly God and truly man, . . . consubstantial with the Father in Godhead, and the same consubstantial with us in manhood, like us in all things except sin; begotten before ages of the Father in Godhead, the same in the last days for us and for our salvation [born] of Mary the virgin *theotokos* in manhood. . . ."[67]

It stood behind the defense of the images in the iconoclastic debates of the eighth century: "Coming down in the flesh, God sanctified created things so that through their humble form God's glory may be seen."[68] It was, as we saw, Luther's favorite paradigm for the anchoring of faith: *Des ew'gen Vaters einig Kind / Jetzt man in der Krippen find. / In unser armes Fleisch und Blut / Verkleidet sich das ewig Gut* (The Father's only Son begot / In the manger has his cot. / In our poor dying flesh and blood / Does mask itself the endless good).[69]

"Incarnation"—we use the term as a household word ourselves without giving much thought to its tenuous beginnings. "The incarnate Word"—it seems such a marvelous shorthand formula for the center of the faith. But is it really anchoring this center *in history?* It speaks of the eternal Word coming down. That is not history. In 1977,

John Hick published a collection of essays under the title, *The Myth of God Incarnate*.[70] The book caused an uproar in the Church of England and beyond. Its seven authors were dubbed "Seven against Christ." In their own eyes, they did not really say anything new. They said what I just said: To an honest historian, there is no compelling historical warrant for this affirmation; it is a myth. One can explain its background, perhaps even its origin; one can retrace its amazing triumph in Christian theology, but at the point of the final contraction, there is no verifiable history. The introductory essay formulated the question that emerged for the authors in this way: Given this situation, could an honest, historically-minded Christianity live without the incarnation? Their answer is yes, but the book is a gloomy book, reflecting the mood of a person's reluctant departure from a cherished childhood home with the grim determination of an adult. It is fascinating to read the editor's report in the 1993 reissue about how the seven have coped with the trauma. Two, in his estimation, have drifted off to the left, one to the right, and four "have gone more or less ahead."[71]

Could Christianity live without the concept of incarnation? Perhaps. The New Testament employs a multiplicity of epithets to describe the significance of that anchor-person in history, Jesus. It has a propensity to regard all and every kind of expectations as being fulfilled in him. The "incarnate Word" is only one of them. But the statement made in this particular formulation is not the point where the final link of Christology with history must be sought. To me it is surprising that the excellent chapter by Frances Young on christological developments in the early church does not refer anywhere to the resurrection and its foundational function for Christology.[72] Granted, the claim that Jesus was raised from the dead (the reverse, so to speak, of the incarnation) is historically not verifiable either. We do not even have canonical accounts of the resurrection itself, only reports about the empty tomb. But historical verification alone does not establish authority. The question is whether the claim can be trusted. Doubts arose early on. Paul tried to answer such doubts in a long argument developed in the famous chapter, 1 Corinthians 15. He opened his discussion with a long list of witnesses from Cephas (Peter) down to himself, naming numerous people to whom the risen Lord had "appeared" in witness to his resurrection, people who had "seen" him, had experienced his presence after Easter (cf. John 20:15, 18, 29). This is different from the possibly expendable *theologoumenon* of the incarnation. While the claim still has to be trusted and authorized by faith, the resurrection message rests on *experience*.

Experience is a big word today. It is *the* great authority in a culture that relies on experience as a potent weapon in the defense both of its own sense of achievement and of its future mission.[73] On the one hand, experience as the quantifiable result of scientific experimentation guarantees the *objectivity* of our view of the world; it defends the facts against conceit and illusion. On the other hand, personal experience guarantees the *subjectivity* of our individual freedom, *my* right to choices and self-determination against imposed demands and external compulsion. This double emphasis on objective and subjective experience as the pillars of our cultural consciousness, self-serving as it is, looked good at a time when the agenda of humanity was the domination of the globe and the subjection of nature. It has far less appeal for a generation that is conscious of living on the brink of apocalyptic catastrophe, at a time when the erosion of human pride in scientific progress makes people unsure of their sense of absolute truth, and their anxiety over the exhausted environment throws doubts on the belief in inalienable human "rights" and their abiding value.

"Experience" is also written large in church and theology today, although it is not necessarily invoked against the use of experience in the culture of our day. As is so often the case, the Christian notion of experience is in large measure the heir and only partly the critic of the culture. Undoubtedly, the decision of younger and older people to consider church-related vocations and to enter seminary is often closely linked to the *experience* of faith in one form or another. To many thoughtful people, the swing of the pendulum in present-day theological education toward a new emphasis on experience is not only welcome; it is long overdue. It is my impression that, in biblical studies, the challenge of this shift in emphasis is particularly serious.

The historical-critical method, once the uncontested single way of life for the guild of biblical exegetes has come under heavy fire in recent years—not so much for what it does, but for what it does not do, for where it is found wanting.

It is perhaps worth listening to one of its sharpest and most eloquent critics in Germany today, Eugen Drewermann.

> Things simply cannot go on in exegesis as before. What is the point of an interpretation of the Bible which does not contain a single authentic feeling, one single deeper insight, anything truly significant? An interpretation of Holy Scripture which actually forbids one to bring along any of one's own feelings or sensibilities, inner tensions and personal questions? How is it possible to hear something of God when the required methodological condition is that one must be concerned exclusively with the genesis of certain religious opinions among certain social constellations of the distant past instead of with God and one's own person? When such an exegesis accompanies the reading of Holy Scripture, it leads a person neither to God nor to him- or herself.[74]

In a catalogue of "four dangers in theology, but especially exegesis," the first danger is "speaking without experience about the experience of others, or: breadwinning scholarship."[75] Drewermann is not much known on this side of the Atlantic; only a few of his numerous books have been translated into English. He is a Roman Catholic priest and academic teacher, and in addition, he publishes as a psychotherapist and an interpreter of Grimm's fairy tales. On the basis of the above quotation, one might be tempted to locate him in the pietist, reactionary milieu of pre-critical Catholic integrism. Nothing would be farther from the truth. The scandal is that Drewermann has been deprived of the right to teach and to function as a priest by the ecclesiastical authorities, because his message has been judged to deny the substance of the Catholic faith, dissolving the biblical data by critical exegesis into a new nature mythology and a much reduced psychologized gospel. As he himself says, "There is no way back behind Bult-mann."[76] Drewermann's admirers—and there are many—regard him as a liberator of the Christian faith from a "neurotic churchyness" (Peter Eicher) and from an inflexible dogmatism to the new freedom of an experiential union of Scripture and inner Spirit. Emotions on both sides are at a high pitch, and the impact of the "Drewermann case" on the future of the Catholic church in Germany is a matter of serious concern for many people inside and outside of that church. Drewermann has said that it was his exposure as a pastor to the intense pain and suffering experienced by the not-so-good Catholics in his care, the doubters, the divorced, the losers, the discouraged and dispairing, that taught him to look at the Bible differently—his experience was the warrant for the challenge he delivered.[77]

It is no secret that recent feminist theology allows experience to play a crucial role as an authorizing power. Representatives of a radical wing do not see how they can grant any authority to the engrained tradition of an oppressive patriarchy, including a patriarchal Bible. These women have given up on Bible and church and are taking their cue from Mary Daly who advocates the organization of sympathizers in marginal communities with an independent life of faith of their own.[78] But even among those who are willing to work from within women-church, that is, the network of feminist women, authority is shifting to experience, *women's* experience. Letty Russell speaks of a new "partnership" of theological sources shared by Scripture, tradition, and historical criticism, but it is the fourth element, experience as the experience of oppressed women, that receives priority.[79] For Elisabeth Schüssler Fiorenza, who still concentrates her professional work on biblical and early Christian sources, the locus of revelation and grace is not in the Bible or the tradition of the patriarchal church, but "in the experience of women . . . struggling for liberation from patriarchy."[80] Rosemary Ruether has been concerned with the need for liturgical expressions of faith within women-church and for a new canon. She sees her *Womenguides,* with its collection of women lore from many sources, as "a handbook from which a new canon might emerge." For her, "human experience is both the starting point and the ending point of the circle of interpretation," including the interpretation of the "prophetic-messianic tradition of the Bible" that establishes the understanding of the faith.[81] Faith obviously must involve experience as an authorizing power. In the present situation, women's experiences must have the right to assert themselves powerfully in women's faith. So, why should experience not be enough as the basis of an authentic faith?

The answer, frankly, must be that experience is *not* enough. There is a fundamental difficulty with the raw material of experience. Experience in itself suffers from ambiguity. It encompasses multiple possibilities. It can lead in many directions, and the deeper it reaches, the more ambiguous it becomes. Take an example: I experience serious illness. Does the experience strengthen my will to live? Does it leave me desperate? Does it intensify or rather destroy my relationship to others? Or an even simpler case: I have a dream. I wake up; the dream, I know, was there, but it is not there any longer and I will soon forget it. It may mean many things, but it has no further existence, no lasting impact if I do not write it down or tell it to someone. Experience needs to be defined, given boundaries, and this form-giving event occurs in *language*. "Out of the abundance of the heart, the mouth speaks" (Matt 12:34). In the light of this simple truth it should not be a surprise that all experiential theologians are rather loquacious—they speak often, and they have much to say. It is a phenomenon worth pondering that the mystics whose experience lifts them to the height of the ineffable feel the greatest urge to speak; mystics are among the most productive writers of the Christian tradition. Saint Augustine "spoke" his experiences into being in his effusive *Confessions*. Since he had the training of a professional rhetorician, he chose his language carefully: It was the language of prayer, of the intimate conversation with the God to whose providence and guidance he attributed every one of his several conversions.

Listening to the Apostle Paul speak about the deepest experience of his life, the encounter with the risen Christ on the road to Damascus, will make clear what I am trying to say. We have Paul's own words about the event in Gal 1:15-16, a brief dependent clause serving a broader argument so that the depth of his statement remains easily unrecognized: "But when the One who had set me apart from my mother's womb and had called me through his grace, was pleased to reveal his Son in me, that I might preach him among the Gentiles. . . ." Paul's Christian self-understanding, his sense of mission, and his life's commitment are expressed in these terse words describing an experience. The question, however, imposes itself right away: what exactly was the "experience"? We do not hear how Paul felt, what he saw or heard—although hearing must have been involved if there was a "call." The later accounts in Acts 9, 22, and 26 supply some details: a vision of light and a voice from heaven, and the iconography of Paul's conversion through the centuries gratefully latched on to this form of the story.[82] Paul himself gives a less dramatic version. "God revealed his Son in me." This terse phrase implies that he already knew the person he was talking about—not personally, but from hearsay. He knew him as the enemy of God, the false messiah who had met his just deserts and whose followers had to be destroyed. But at that moment near Damascus, he began to know him differently, that is, as the Son of God—a new epithet for the same person. There is still much debate among exegetes over the background of the term "Son of God." But "Son" is different from "enemy"—radically different, like light from darkness, life from death. Paul's conversion involved a total change of language with all its radical consequences. This is the point: Experience needs definition; it seeks expression. Even more succinctly: experience is aimed at language. Faith, precisely experiential faith, cannot avoid language. Human language is the special privilege of our species. It gives experience the form through which it acquires reality. Language is our access to reality; one might argue that it stands above reality because language can express even that which is unreal, that which *is not*. Throughout the history of philosophy, there has been an interest in a metaphysics of language right down to Heidegger's "language as the house of being."

Thus, faith, real faith, needs its language. Without language, it has no existence. And this language, whatever its specific shape, has a clear priority in the sequence of existence. Language is already there, prior to experience. Paul uses the language of his contemporary religious environment when he describes the experience of his conversion with the words: "to *reveal his Son* in me." In a treatise entitled "On the Teacher" (*De Magistro*), Augustine left us the report of a wonderful conversation he had with his teenage son, Adeodatus.[83] Augustine does not pose as a metaphysician of language, but he leads the young man to admit a number of simple points: language is a convention among humans, a system of signs that mean something because humans agreed that they should; this system is learned on authority, and authority alone, from our mothers as the "mother tongue"; and finally, the conviction that what it says is true can only come by experience, through the "inward teacher," whom Augustine identifies with Christ, the *Logos,* the Word of God. Faith needs language in order to be, and it needs experience to move from the mere sound of words to their truth.

Christian faith, too, has its language. There is something like a Christian "mother tongue" for faith we have learned from our mothers and fathers in the faith. This language certainly needs the inward teacher in order to become "true" for us; but it is present already as a specific accumulation of terms that together form a coherent tale— the expression, and at the same time the nourishment, of the experience of generations, the language of the community of faith through history.

When George Lindbeck, a veteran of many ecumenical dialogues, wanted to write a book on the question of why partners in such dialogues can say that they have reached reconciliation on formerly divisive doctrines and yet claim full continuity with their separate doctrinal identities, he found that he had to write on something much more fundamental, far more basic. He had to write on *The Nature of Doctrine,* even the nature of religion itself.[84] The answer he finally gave to the question rested on the conviction that a religion, namely, the distinctive identity of a coherent group of believers, is a "kind of cultural and/or linguistic framework or medium that shapes the entirety of life and thought." "Like a culture or language, it is a communal phenomenon that shapes the subjectivities of individuals rather than being primarily a manifestation of those subjectivities. It comprises a vocabulary of discursive and non-discursive symbols together with a distinctive logic or grammar in terms of which this vocabulary can be meaningfully deployed."[85] In a rather elaborate and sophisticated formulation, this is what I mean when I refer to the "mother tongue" of Christian faith.

CHAPTER 3

The Creative Word of God:
Tradition and Interpretation

"God's word runs swiftly." *(Psalm 147:15)*

W<small>E SPOKE OF THE</small> C<small>HRISTIAN MOTHER TONGUE, THE LINGUISTIC WEB THAT</small> gives meaning to experience and reality, through which a person is "made" a Christian, either by growing up in the community of faith or by being socialized into it later. This mother tongue has a variety of expressions. In the tradition of our churches it comes first in the form of confessions of faith or *creeds.* The Greek word for "creed" is *symbolon,* symbol. "Symbols" can be brief, very brief—just one phrase, one christological title, as we noted in Paul's description of his new-found faith (Gal 1:16). Oscar Cullmann has observed that the earliest Christian confessions were brief, simple statements, always with a christological core, but frequently expanded into binitarian or trinitarian phrases (e.g., 1 Cor 8:6; 2 Cor 13:14).[86] Paul already cited several of them from the earliest Christian tradition before him, for instance in Phil 2:11: ". . .that every tongue should confess that Jesus Christ is Lord." Such brief creeds were not dispensable verbiage. They had power.

Indeed, symbols were critical: they could divide whole worlds; one phrase could spell life or death. Paul leaves no doubt about that: "No one speaking by the Spirit of God ever says 'Jesus be cursed!' and no one can say 'Jesus is Lord!' except by the Holy spirit" (1 Cor 12:3). This is not a future-directed, apocalyptic warning; it is a reference to the actual choice between life and death that Christians faced in times of persecution. There was more than one time in the history of the church when subscription to a creed spelled peace or exile, honor or execution. Creedal language may well be the primary form of the Christian mother tongue for faith. Paul enforces this impression when he uses the vocabulary of "receiving" and "handing on" in connection with the brief creedal statements he quotes: "I delivered to you. . . what I also received" (1 Cor 15:3). This is the language of tradition—from the Latin word *tradere,* "to hand on"—and "handing on" is what mothers do with language. In the early centuries, the "handing on" of the baptismal creed was a special event during the preparation of candidates for baptism. It occurred a few weeks before Easter in a liturgical setting, and the sources for this rite, which was called the "handing on of the creed" (*traditio symboli*), still give evidence of the deep respect with which these precious words were handled. In solemn procession, four deacons, preceded by candlebearers and thurifers, would bring the books of the four Gospels forward and deposit them on the four corners of the altar. Then the words of the creed were explained and rehearsed, the bishop intoning them with a clear voice.[87]

We are talking here already about another form of the mother tongue, *the liturgy.* In all religions, liturgical language is one of the most tenacious forms of tradition, always resisting change. Through many of the liturgical phrases we use in our Lutheran worship service today, we are in direct contact with the Christians of the early centuries. The "Preface," for instance, that little dialogue that occurs in the liturgy of the Supper ("Lift up your hearts! We lift them to the Lord! Let us give thanks to the Lord our God! It is meet and right so to do!") is found with the very same words in the Roman liturgy as far back as the year 200 C.E.

Of course, hymnody has always been an important part of the liturgical mother tongue. Good hymns are not meant merely to provide an atmosphere, to stir emotions and feelings. They express the faith in words—and what a wealth of words they offer! My mother sang many hymns with us children, and we expanded our vocabulary by learning many a strange and unusual word this way. In the early Lutheran churches, hymnals were printed without music. They were used not only in church but also as teaching aids and prayer books for home devotions. As such, there was room in them for many more hymns than in their modern counterparts, hymns adapted to every conceivable situation in the life of an individual or a family: hymns for the seasons of the church year, for morning, noontime, and evening as well as for all kinds of adversities and celebrations. My great-grandfather published such a hymnal for the deaconess home in Dresden where he was the pastor and director in 1872; the number of hymns he included did not quite match that of the year, but it came close: 1836.[88]

It was a joy to see that *Lutheran Book of Worship*, published in 1975, included twenty of Luther's thirty-six hymns, compared with only seven in the old *Service Book and Hymnal* of 1958. In the early Lutheran hymnals, Luther's hymns, grouped together, occupied a place of honor; they always opened the collection. *LBW* obviously wanted to encourage the use of this treasure trove. My only regret is that many texts have been "devotionalized" in their new English translation, losing much of their theological bite. To give an example: Earlier in these lectures, I was unable to use the *LBW* translation of stanza two of Luther's Christmas hymn, "All praise to you, eternal Lord," because the words printed there do not convey what Luther said.[89] Luther's hymns were carriers of his theology; their intention was to *teach* as well as to edify. Not all of them were occasional poems, as is frequently assumed. In his later years, Luther made a conscious effort to provide a hymn for each part of his catechism, and these hymns were long and substantial. Only two of them made it into *LBW*.[90]

The *Catechism* is yet another form of the Christian language of faith. The Reformation movement made catechisms the universal vehicle for instruction in the faith.[91] Luther's Small Catechism has five parts: the Ten Commandments, the Creed, the Lord's Prayer, Baptism, and the Supper, in this order. It is concise, carefully worded, and was meant to be illustrated by woodcuts. Among the early printed versions were large posters to be hung in the home as a help for the expected memorization as well as the practice of reading skills— comparable to the ABC posters in school. The catechism's very structure reflects a clear *theological* argument: First comes the law, then the gospel, then the answer of faith in the Lord's Prayer, and finally the visible signs of the sacraments sealing the verbal promise.

Yes, *theology* is a form of the Christian mother tongue for faith also. Karl Barth defined academic theology, "in distinction from the 'theology' of the simple testimony of faith and life and the 'theology' of the service of God," as the "scientific self-examination of the Christian Church with respect to the content of its distinctive talk about God."[92] Theology is not the everyday language of faith, the language of worship and prayer. It is a secondary, expanded form of that language that tries to spell out the wider implications, keep up the conversation with contemporary thought, and learn from its methodology. Theological tradition is not handed down in the form of a specific language of its own but remains an ever-present *task* for each generation—the task of scrutinizing, verifying, weighing, updating all the other forms of expression that faith experience is creating in the church, with a view toward making them understandable in the framework of contemporary culture.

Experiential faith in our day and age will not have much of a problem with the primary form of the mother tongue, creedal language. As has often been pointed out, even the very personal testimonies at revival meetings tend to follow a standard format; there is a clear "rhetoric of conversion" even in the most experientially oriented circles. But liturgy? Many people have no qualms singing hymns in church, especially the kind they like; but their experiential faith often hesitates when it confronts the formal liturgical language of a traditional worship service. Not all drifters who are coming into a Lutheran congregation from other denominations appreciate it: "Well, you know, that eleven o'clock service is *so* ceremonious!" Seriously, does traditional liturgical language not stifle the freedom of expression, the spontaneous urgings of the Spirit? Is there not the danger of thoughtless repetition? When it comes to the language of the catechism, the hesitation is apt to grow even stronger. "Teaching the catechism"—is this not the imposition of a merely formulaic faith, the inculcation of a docile receptivity? Are there no problems with rote memorization and required regurgitation of content? And theology—what use does the person in the pew have for it? Students and teachers in our seminaries often have a hard time explaining to outsiders, even to sincere church-goers, what they actually "do" in theology classes. The persistent suspicion is that the academic routine in those settings may be nothing more than an exercise in useless speculation, divisive bickering, and ridiculous hairsplitting.

The suspicions are perhaps not totally unfounded, and the dangers are real. But we need to remember that all forms of the mother tongue for faith go back to one matrix ("matrix" is a Latin word derived from *mater*, "mother"): the mother soil is Scripture. Creeds are intended to function as summaries of the biblical witness, the liturgy in all its parts lives from the biblical Word to nourish the inner "senses" of the participants, catechisms were written to make the biblical Word teachable, and theology as a scientific enterprise grew out of the practice of raising and answering "questions" in the biblical courses of the medieval schools and universities.[93] Scripture as the common matrix, the mother soil of all forms of the Christian mother tongue—might this be the answer to the search of experiential faith for its language? Not some derived norm, but the source; not tradition, but Scripture alone? Should the church simply call for a return to the innocent biblicism of the good old days? This possibility alone may sound ominous to people who are eager to move on in church and society. They will be glad to hear that there are problems with Scripture as the ultimate language for faith as well.

We want to say that it is *God* who speaks in Scripture. This is the meaning of the doctrine of inspiration, as we saw. The Bible is not just literature like any other book. But God *speaks*. An inspired Bible does not solve any problems we as hearers and readers might have with its content; on the contrary, it opens up the real problem, which is language itself. God *speaks*. This means: God uses language, our language, a clearly human phenomenon, and thereby puts the deity at the mercy of our language's rules and limitations. We said earlier that experience is ambiguous, and therefore it aims at language. Language is not ambiguous in the same sense. But it is not unambiguous either.

It can reveal and it can hide; it can speak the truth and it can pronounce a lie; it can heal and it can hurt. As a human phenomenon, language is always imperfect, groping, vulnerable; it can be misunderstood, misused, manipulated. It participates in the openness of all human speech, which must be filled with specific meaning through specific human experience. As a record of past experience with God, the Bible will never replace the need for personal faith experience today. It never says it all. But the Bible, its stories, its prayers, its visions, its admonitions can help my personal experience find its language; it can interpret *me*. Biblical language does not come as a monolithic block of truth from which any busybody can quarry bits and pieces for his or her own agenda. It is not a meteorite of "holy material" concealing a system of "Bible doctrines" that the theologians must tease out. Biblical language in all its various forms is an invitation to our faith—nothing more, but also nothing less.

Treating biblical language as an invitational language—this indeed would be a "biblicism" I might advocate in our situation today. If the God of the Bible did not speak in the "tongue of angels" (1 Cor 13:1), which he certainly could have done, but instead employed human speech and language in all its vulnerability—a miracle of love no less astonishing than that of the incarnation!—then it is clear that God does not want to compel or force us into anything, to ram any language down our throat. The language of the Bible in its many forms is as tentative, as fragile, as experimental as any human speech to which we listen every day. It is sitting there, gently extending an invitation to our experience and to our faith, as confident and self-assured or timid and struggling as it may be: Come in! Settle down! Make yourself at home! Of course, the convenient thing about invitations is that they can be turned down. We often turn down an invitation because it takes time away from more important preoccupations or because we think we have more appealing alternatives. In this case, do we really have a good alternative? One thing is clear from the experience of millions of people throughout the centuries. If we accept this invitation, we are in for a long, long party, not just a brief happening. Entering the house of biblical language takes us into a process, an unending process of learning.

It is like learning any language—French, Chinese, Swahili—any foreign system of speech. There is much drudgery connected with the process: rote memorization, repetition, exercise, listening to tapes, to teachers. It takes much time and effort. But once you are fully into it, once you feel at home, the fun begins; the reality of the language world you have entered envelopes you and slowly expands the horizons of your previous world. You begin to understand, to dialogue, to weigh your words, to play with phrases and their meaning. You find yourself participating in an entirely new game. It is hard to be against memory training, repetition, exercise, and listening to authorities when you want to learn languages. Certainly, these are not the only methods, and people have different styles of learning. Augustine speaks with admiration of "Antony, the holy and perfect Egyptian monk, who is said to have memorized the Sacred Scriptures simply by hearing them."[94] I admit that I am somewhat skeptical here. If Antony really knew the entire Bible by heart, or even some parts, there probably was more drudgery involved than Augustine allowed for or was aware of: listening, listening again, repeating.

What impresses me more is the attempt of a medieval schoolmaster such as Hugh of St. Victor, who endeavored to help the choir boys under his care with the mechanics of memorizing the Latin Psalter—a formidable task by our standards, but a normal expectation in monastery and school at that time. Be methodical, he said; learn the psalms in sequence, one after the other, but do not try to remember them just by numbers—it will not work. Always repeat the number together with the first words: Psalm 1, *Beatus vir;* Psalm 2, *Quare fremuerunt;* Psalm 3, *Domine quid multiplicati sunt.* In this way, the abstract sequence of numbers will be supported by something more tangible and recollectable.[95] Martin Luther reports that, when the true meaning of the "righteousness of God" in Rom 1:17 dawned on him in his famous "tower experience," he "ran through the Scriptures from memory"—obviously to check other occurrences of the term.[96] Did he use a concordance? I doubt it. Like other monks and students of the Bible, he apparently had a rather precise recall of large portions of the biblical text. We probably need to make far more serious efforts to live with the Bible day by day ourselves if we want to hand on to future generations any measure of the biblical literacy exhibited by our ancestors in the faith, not to mention their insights into the practice of the Christian life, which tends to come naturally with this routine.

Part of the wonderful "playing" that a person might do once his or her faith is sufficiently at home in the language of the Bible would be the fuller exploration of those other forms of the mother tongue that we considered earlier on. It is exciting for a thinking person to observe how creeds grew, how liturgies developed and changed, how theology sometimes drew closer, sometimes farther away from the biblical mother soil and why. You will have to forgive a church historian for naming this kind of excitement first. Working in this field brings much joy. When I was teaching a seminary course on "Main themes of Christian doctrine," I quickly discovered that I could not begin with the Nicene Creed or the Chalcedonian Decree in their ponderous language garb, which, at first hearing, is so foreign to the modern mind. I had to walk my students, step by step, down the entire painful road of people's faith experience expressed in the "symbols" of the New Testament to the creedal formulas of the fourth and fifth centuries in order to give that odd language a chance to be grasped and understood. How can one know what "of one substance with the Father" means if one has not wrestled with a considerable amount of creative biblical thinking on substance, deity, time and eternity from the Gospel of John in the Bible via Irenaeus and Origen down to Arius and Athanasius in the fourth century? How can you explain to anyone why we confess Christ "truly God and truly human" if you have never watched anxiously the seesaw of biblical argumentation between Alexandria and Antioch, Cyril and Nestorius? There are, of course, more practical ways of exploring and sampling the world of the biblical matrix. More than 100,000 people from all over the world, most in their teens and twenties, participated in the Taizé Gathering in Paris in January 1995.[97] They sang the simple songs of the Taizé Brothers, listened to plain words of testimony, prayed together the collects of the ancient liturgies—all of these forms of faith speech arising from the scriptural words of the tradition and creating a new community of trust where people who had never seen each other understood not only each other's answers but also the questions behind the answers, the longings of their hearts, and the depth of their search for meaning.

If our experiential faith can discover, learn, and appropriate the biblical language as its own, the reverse sequence is equally possible: Bible reading, Bible study, Bible preaching certainly can and do lead to the experience of faith and its renewal, even to new "conversions" on our pilgrimage of faith. *Fides ex auditu,* "Faith comes from what is heard" (Rom 10:17). This, of course, was the preferred strategy of the Reformers; they made sure that everyone could hear—in the vernacular. It was also the basis of Christian missionary preaching in Kenneth Scott Latourette's "Great Century" of Christian expansion, the nineteenth and the early twentieth.[98] Missionaries went out "to preach Christ" to the nations, hoping for faith to arise in the wake of this activity, for lives to change, and for community to be created. It often worked, but just as often it did not. We may doubt the need for the priority of this sequence today in a climate of interreligious encounter. We may want to begin the other way around, as we have been discussing here, starting from the faith experience people claim as their own and finding the bridge to the biblical mother tongue along the road of the dialogue. Wherever we start, however, the framework will remain the same: the life-sustaining exchange between experienced faith and the Bible is a rhythmic movement, a breathing in and a breathing out; the exchange happens within the same house. And when faith goes out to meet the challenges of the day, it must come home from all its excursions to the matrix—the language of the Bible.

In a thoughtful article on "Scripture and Experience," Gerhard Ebeling showed how deeply this rhythm is embedded in Luther's theology.[99] There is no contradiction to the rule of *sola scriptura* here. *Sola scriptura* is not a "formal principle," even in the sense in which Lutheran orthodoxy proposed it. It does not introduce a second restrictive selection beyond the notion of the canon. It does not exclude other texts and issues from being considered; their challenge belongs to the material of one's theologizing so that Scripture will have a chance to prove its worth in the comparison. *Sola scriptura* is not a license to atomize Scripture's content into arbitrary chunks of prooftexts to which one clings obstinately as a weapon and warrant in one's self-chosen fights. For Luther, Ebeling suggests, *sola scriptura* had the function of pointing to the circular motion in which both the work of interpreting Scripture and the work of formulating theology toward the outside from Scripture must be undertaken. In this sense, scripture is its own interpreter—*scriptura sui ipsius interpres*. Interpretation and reformulation happen in the same house. "Scripture interprets itself inasmuch as it alone is the source of the attitude of living with it fruitfully. That is the meaning of the *sola scriptura* formula to which the other exclusive phrases [grace alone, faith alone, Christ alone] give greater precision, especially the *solus Christus*. Only such a concentration allows for the freedom and open-minded approach which characterize Luther's use of the Bible."[100] Luther was free enough to derive from his intensive life with the Bible and his constant exegetical endeavors the authority to risk bold new formulations in preaching, to propose scope and form of new doctrine even against old tradition, and to call Christians high and low to specific, often controversial action. It belongs to this freedom that, in speaking from the biblical matrix in this way, Luther could also call bluntly on experience to serve as his second authority. In a sermon on 1 Corinthians 15, he notes Paul's two categories of "witnesses" for the proclamation of the resurrection: Scripture and the appearances of the risen Lord, that is, experience. "In the same way, I too can preach about the faith through God's grace because I have on my side both scripture, and then also experience."[101] Experience here is not simply sense experience, world experience, or "special revelation" (in the same sermon Luther thunders mightily against the *Schwärmer*) but "conscience-experience" as Ebeling calls it, the inner witness of the Spirit triggered by Scripture that God has accepted me despite hell, devil, death, and my own powerlessness. Doctrine has become personal conviction and vice versa—one cannot ask which came first in this experience. There is a lesson in this. The witness of Scripture as the Word of God can be handed on only together with that of one's own conscience-experience. It is the integration of the two, Scripture and experience, that calls for and authorizes the bold new statement of faith which we must attempt time and again in our preaching and teaching, tearing down and building up.

Gerhard Ebeling has deepened this argument in an article that appeared in 1994, "Hermeneutics between the Power of the Word of God and Its De-Powerment in Our Modern Age."[102] Once again, Martin Luther provides a point of orientation. For Luther, the power of the Word of God in Scripture manifests itself in a peculiar way, in an antithetical movement characterized by several hermeneutical shifts, inversions, or reversals. The first reversal has to do with the reader's laborious and at first frustrating wrestling with a hard text, an experience that now and then ends on the opposite note, in the joyful and liberating experience of being overpowered by the text. "Note that the power of Scripture is of this kind: Scripture is not being conformed to the one who studies Scripture but transforms into itself and its powers the one who loves it."[103] This is a very early quotation, and the phenomenon is well known. If one replaces "the readers" by the extratextual world they bring with them to the task, George Lindbeck's notion of "intratextuality" may well be describing the same dynamic: "Intratextual theology redescribes reality within the scriptural framework rather than translating scripture into extrascriptural categories. It is the text so to speak which absorbs the world, rather than the world the text."[104]

The second reversal occurs within the Scriptures themselves speaking to us as the Word of God. It is a reversal in the function of this Word being pondered and experienced. God's Word shifts from being law to being gospel, from killing to making alive, in a single motion. Only through the old self dying can the new self be raised. Lutherans know this truth. Rightly dividing the law and the gospel makes the theologian.[105] This is not a matter of distributing law and gospel by texts: today's lesson is law; next Sunday's will be gospel. Nor is it a matter of figuring out the proper dosage of each in counseling and pastoral work. Sensitivity certainly is needed in all branches of pastoral care, but it is not enough if it is sensitivity to the human situation into which the Word is spoken; it must be in equal measure sensitivity to the awesome power of the Word itself which does not only sound forth but performs. This reversal within Scripture itself is difficult to grasp. Lutheran theologians have time and again attempted to describe it in new ways. Its understanding has not become easier, though. In the Lutheran-Roman Catholic Dialogue document, "Justification by Faith" (1985), a special section on "A Lutheran Hermeneutical Perspective" had to be added because there seemed to be no other way to integrate the phenomenon into a common language.[106]

The third reversal occurs in the turn from the written to the oral word, from Scripture to Proclamation, the "living voice of the gospel" (*viva vox evangelii*) with which we began our first lecture. Ebeling points out that, for Luther, "there is an essential affinity between Scripture and the Law." The written page means distance; there is permanence, a stern once-for-allness. The gospel, on the other hand, is at bottom not a written phenomenon. It is "good news, to be published not with the pen, but with the mouth," to be poured into public hearing with a living voice.[107] With all his love and reverence for the Scriptures, Luther was amazingly clear about their secondary character and their origin as a kind of emergency measure:

> "That one had to write books is already a great deterioration and a limitation of the spirit dictated by necessity—it is not the way of the New Testament; for instead of devout preachers there arose heretics, false teachers and sundry errors which give to the sheep of Christ poison instead of pasture. Therefore one must do all one can, make the most determined effort to save at least some sheep from the wolves; and thus it was that people began to write and through writing, in so far as that was possible, to lead the little sheep into the scriptures, so that they could feed themselves and be protected from the wolves."[108]

"In the New Testament the sermon should orally and publicly take place with living voice and bring into speech and hearing what was before concealed in the letter and secret visions. . . . Christ himself did not put down his teaching in writing as Moses had done, but he proclaimed it orally and also commanded that it be continued orally, and gave no command that it be written down. The apostles wrote very little. In fact, not all of them wrote . . . and even those who did write did nothing more than direct us into the old scriptures just as the angel directed the shepherds to the manger and the diapers, and the star led those magi to Bethlehem! Therefore, it is not at all according to the New Testament to write books about Christian teaching—but instead of books there should be in all places good, learned, zealous and devout preachers who would draw the living Word out of the old writings and constantly impress it upon the people as did the apostles."[109]

These are very astute observations in an age of a triumphant culture of the book. They arose as theological insights from an intensive life with the Bible, but they also point to a historical phenomenon of great importance: the priority of orality in human culture. Walter Ong, who has written a fascinating book on this subject (*Orality and Literacy: The Technologizing of the Word,* 2d ed., 1988), reminds us that "we have been oral far longer than we have been literate." Western literature, we say, began with Homer. But Homer's epic poems had no written originals. Homer was a bard, a professional singer of tales of the kind Albert Lord still found in modern Balkan countries.[110] In his *Phaidros,* Plato has Socrates tell the story about an inventor who presented to a wise Egyptian king several of his "inventions" such as numbers, measures, the basics of astronomy, and an alphabet.[111] When he praised the usefulness of his letters, the king's reaction was less than enthusiastic. The invention, he argued, was quite useless. Written words sit there, helpless and exposed to everyone's whim; they cannot talk back or defend themselves. Rather than replacing memory, they only remind us of that which is already in the memory. And they never say anything different—how boring! What is this compared with the living *logos,* the spoken word that issues from its author's heart and knows where it is going—flexible, adaptable to the situation; truth backed up by a personality!

Jesus did not write. We do not have one written line from him. In his understanding of authority, even Paul reflects the priority of orality over literacy. He did regard the Hebrew Scriptures as authoritative. But the higher authority for him was a word of the *Kyrios* and the oral tradition that had been handed down to him. Second Corinthians 10:10 reveals one of Paul's most serious shortcomings in the eyes of his critics: he was strong in his letters but weak in his personal appearance and oral performance. When Papias, one of the early Apostolic Fathers, explains the intention of his "Exposition of Dominical Oracles," he says that he tried to gather as much oral information as he could from the "elders" who had heard the teaching of the apostles: "For I assumed that what is derived from books does not profit me so much as what is derived from a living and abiding voice."[112] Papias thinks of authentic, reliable tradition in the way in which the traditions of philosophical schools in antiquity continued the *auctoritas* of their founders. Clement of Alexandria refers repeatedly to the "tradition" of his own revered teacher, Pantaenus, who headed the school at Alexandria but did not leave so much as a line in writing. "The presbyters did not write" he states laconically.[113] Tertullian mentions some Christians who thought that a written oath in a business contract did not fall under Jesus' prohibition to swear an oath; their reason: it was "only" written.[114]

For us, this logic is hard to understand. Luther suggested that the written New Testament came into being as a means of defense against heresy. He probably was not far from the mark. Secret oral tradition was the authority invoked by Christian Gnostic groups. Trying to refute such claims, Irenaeus made use of the writings of the Christian movement, not because they were written and therefore more reliable, but because they were public, not secret. He too drew on the "living word" of the oral tradition: The rule of faith and the bishop in apostolic tradition stood together with the writings as public witnesses to the truth of his tradition.[115]

Walter Ong listed the consequences of the shift from an oral to a literate culture: Loss of the power of memory and of the old systems of mnemonic aids; loss of flexibility in assigning dates; development of graphic helps for orientation on a written scroll or page; and the necessity of all kinds of textual aids to help recall. The invention of printing was the final step in moving human consciousness away from the oral roots of language. Abstract, rigidly delimited, linear forms of thinking and speaking replaced the old situational, open-ended, and flexible ones. Are we returning to "orality" in our days? There are some indications that seem to point in this direction. For fifty years in this century, people lived in a radio culture, exposed to an oral form of communication that revolutionized their assimilation of news and their articulation of a sense of participation in the world. During the same period, the telephone brought the demise of a whole culture of letter-writing that had reached its peak in the early 1900s. Professor Adolph von Harnack received mail three times daily in early twentieth-century Berlin and could answer a morning letter from a colleague the same afternoon. Contemporary biographical research can no longer rely on a stack of letters as primary sources; today's celebrities may not have written more than a few real letters during their lifetime. In our schools, we assign fewer and fewer readings from textbooks, which are getting slimmer and slimmer; much of the actual learning takes place in group discussions and face-to-face encounters. Teaching skills have become an important criterion in appointments, and students flock to reputedly good lecturers. I was struck by a remark Yves Congar penned in a memorial for the Aquinas scholar Marie-Dominique Chenu in 1975, meaning to excuse the great scholar for not having published more than he did: "When the religious history of this century will be written one day, one will have to consider the personal impact people had. The dissemination of ideas today happens in large measure through personal contact and individual charism. Oral teaching occupies as important a place as written."[116]

There is truth in these observations, but the impression of a
return to orality is probably an illusion. Some of us remember the
publication of Marshall McLuhan's book, *The Gutenberg Galaxy: The
Making of Typographic Man* in 1961. Using his "mosaic" approach to
media studies, McLuhan described the immense intellectual changes
introduced by the art of printing. More importantly, however, he
announced the end of that old "galaxy" of Gutenberg's art and the
beginning of a new era, the electronic age. If, in McLuhan's estimation, we had reached the Elizabethan Age after Gutenberg in 1962,
we probably are in the vicinity of the French Revolution by now. The
characteristics of our new media culture are obvious: The immediacy
of the spoken and printed word has been eclipsed by the immediacy
of vision; it may be helpful to recall that vision was regarded as the
most authoritative of the five bodily senses already in the Middle
Ages. Today, the range of authentic images of reality conveyed by the
mass media has become so overwhelming that there is no time any
more to digest, sort out, and order the sense impressions—which
would be the proper activity of the intellect according to Thomas
Aquinas. But intellectual effort is not in great demand; it is discouraged by the very shows that are most popular on TV. Thus, we just
take in the stimuli and are left with little more than our instincts and
emotions to cope with the truth of visual information. This is in no
way a return to Plato's orality, which was based on interpersonal
exchange, on give and take, persuasion and the common search for
truth.

In fact, we seem to be living in an age of unprecedented devaluation of the word, written as well as oral. This devaluation comes in
two forms. The first is inflation. Too many words are descending on us
all the time: advertising, aggressive solicitation, political rhetoric,
papers, magazines, novels on the bestseller list. We are overexposed
and react protectively. "It's just rhetoric." "Promises, promises!" "Mere
talk; words, nothing but words." The second form of the devaluation
is reduction. With this term, I want to point to the frightening signs
of the oppressive literalism that has become so pervasive in recent
years. One must read the small print in every contract, word for word;

it determines what one can hope or fear; it decides one's future. You may be sued over a single word or phrase you uttered, and by the same token for its omission. I miss one stroke on the keyboard, and my computer comes back with the humiliating message: "You made an error. There is no such term." There used to be some leeway in language, some room to play and experiment. This seems no longer to be the case. Language has become dead serious.

What is the reason for this double devaluation of the word? I do not think it is a general annoyance with, or distrust of, words. We are comfortable with their omnipresence. We have learned to use, manipulate, and "read" words, and we have figured out ways to decide when they are serious or alarming. We are aware of their limitations and their usefulness. Methods of interpretation have brought home to us the ambiguity of all words, but we have grown accustomed to living with pluralism in our world. Rather, the devaluation of the word stems from the distrust of the *auctores* of words, the human minds behind them: *Omnis homo mendax*—all humans are liars.[117] This is a biblical pronouncement. It is also a general truth that imposes itself more powerfully today than at any other point in time. We have lost faith in humanity.

Where does all of this leave the Bible? In a way, it is caught in the middle. Insofar as the Bible is literature, even a classic,[118] a collection of books by human authors, the loss of faith in humanity must affect it. If we treat the Bible within the parameter of our human world exclusively, we have every reason to begin with a "hermeneutics of suspicion"— it will be amply vindicated. One can easily understand the reaction of women readers who find the book hopelessly patriarchal, put it aside, and concentrate on building their spiritual home elsewhere. The church of Christ is certainly not the "church of man." But it is not only women-church, or the church of any special-experience group either, as important as special experience, special concerns, and special gifts are. The church is the creation of God's Word, called out of a wealth of diverse human experiences as an inclusive, pluralistic group of people, men and women of all races and nations—the kind of group which we want to be. Wishes do not suffice, however.

Where, in the past, the dignity of other cultures, other faiths, other people has been disregarded, repentance and forgiveness are needed so that trust can grow again. Such a worldwide, reconciled church will be the one that can reckon with an *auctor* of Scripture who does not have to be mistrusted like another human but can be supremely trusted. For this church, the Bible will be the house in which the breathing-in will be done, the concentration on the center of faith— the story of Jesus Christ; and where the breathing-out will have its beginning as well, the "living word" in witness and proclamation.

It may be obvious enough that I have considerable sympathy for a theology of story or, more precisely, for a narrative theology that is being explored by numerous theologians today. In the preface to the 1992 edition of his *Models of Revelation,* Avery Dulles classified Hans Frei, George Lindbeck, David Kelsey, and Ron Thiemann under his model IV, "Revelation as Dialectical Presense," which, in the earlier edition, was represented by Karl Barth, Emil Brunner, and Rudolf Bultmann. This intriguing expansion of the group is fine with me. I have learned from all of these people. Hans Frei exposed the consequences of the "eclipse of the biblical narrative" over the past two hundred years and called, first implicitly, then explicitly for this narrative's restoration. [119] This is what a number of Frei's students are now advocating. The return to story may be the proper framework for a revaluation of the word, at least within the house of the Christian church, and for a revival of the pregnant orality of the Christian mother tongue. Much storytelling, both from the biblical materials and from the Christian conscience-experience will be needed to allow the invitational character of the biblical language to exercise its creative function.

In my reading, I have come across an article by Minka Shura Sprague. [120] The author argues that a careful reading of biblical stories with the tools of critical scholarship can liberate traditions from their time-bound biblical context and permit an authentic retelling in and for our time. Sprague's imaginative retelling of the Noah story is provocative enough to "shape it into a new story for dialogue in another community." Of course, biblical narrative occurs not only in the so-called historical books of the Bible. This is why I thought of a Psalm word as a motto for this final lecture: "God's word runs swiftly" (Ps 147:15). The researcher who tries to trace important doctrinal developments encounters here one of the instances where the hypostatization, the personification of the Word of God is anchored in the Jewish tradition.[121] In the Christian tradition, as we have seen, this personalization had its place in the debates over Christology. What a story in this verse! I hear it in one breath with Isaiah 55:11, a classic expression of the performative nature of the Word's activity: "So shall my word be that goes out from my mouth: it shall not return to me empty, but it shall accomplish that which I purpose and succeed in the thing for which I sent it." I also think of the unforgettable image in Julian of Norwich's *Showings:* the humble servant, old and new Adam in one, standing by the throne in the wilderness, running off eagerly to do his work, falling, writhing in pain, under the loving gaze of his lord.[122] Or of the story-image in the fifth stanza of Luther's hymn, "Dear Christians, one and all rejoice," a true ballad of justification if there ever was one: "God said to his beloved Son: / 'Tis time to have compassion. / Then run, bright jewel of my crown / And bring to all salvation. / From sin and sorrow set them free, / Slay bitter death for them that they / May live with you forever."[123] The words of Luther's hymn are an invitation for the one who sings them to identify with the story, to find words for his or her own faith experience, and to go on from there living it out. We need to listen in the story for the story, which will be ours in its full force of judgment and grace if we breathe in with it and breathe out again. This is what it would mean to hear God's Word in the Bible.

Let me close with two testimonies that are as personal as they are theological. Letty Russell wrote in 1985: "For me, the Bible is 'scripture,' because it functions as 'script' or prompting for life. Its authority in my life stems from its story of God's invitation to participation in the wholeness, peace, and justice in the world. Responding to this invitation has made it my own story, or script, through the power of the Spirit at work in communities of struggle and faith." And, once again, Gerhard Ebeling in 1994: "From the Word faith emerges, and from faith word again, in ever new acts of interpreting and directing the Gospel—in such a way, however, that any such language event always returns to its (biblical) origin in order to come forth from it purified to enter again the ever-changing course of time." According to the Acts of the Apostles, Paul said in his speech at Athens, probably quoting a phrase from the philosophical tradition: "In God we live and move and have our being" (Acts 17:28). For him as for us, this God is the God of language and speech (*Deus loquens*) who keeps inviting us into the world of the biblical story in its totality if we are in search for meaning—the meaning of our own experience and the experience of those whom we are called to serve.

By Terence E. Fretheim

Professor Froehlich's approach to this topic is obviously quite distinct from my own. This reflects our different disciplines and theological commitments as well as our somewhat differing understandings of the Bible as the Word of God. I lift up a few matters where his considerations touch my own.

Froehlich assumes that biblical authority is in a state of crisis in our time and that this crisis is a "neuralgic point, perhaps *the* neuralgic point" for the churches (p. 6). Speaking as a church historian, and drawing masterfully on the resources of the ecclesiastical tradition, he seeks to ameliorate the crisis through a recovery of appropriate understandings of the Word of God as inspired, incarnate, and creative. In the process, he discusses the major themes associated with biblical authority.

While I essentially agree with his discernment of the critical situation regarding the Bible, I cannot always agree with his response.

In introducing this undertaking, Froehlich develops a helpful understanding of authority as relational (and practical and functional), as that which one has reason to trust (p. 14). This can be linked with my considerations regarding the trustworthiness of certain biblical claims, particularly those regarding God (see especially chapter 5 below). I concluded that there are some biblical statements about God (as well as other matters) to which the reader simply has to say No! Readers can no longer simply trust everything that the Bible says, about God as well as other matters, and this makes problematic such an understanding of authority. I do think the language of trust can continue to be helpful, but if we are to use it, we will have to understand trust as something less than absolute. We commonly do this in speaking of interhuman relationships. Again and again, human beings place their trust in persons who are less than perfect, who on occasion or often fail. We must face a comparable understanding of the Bible without equivocation: the Bible at times fails us, even regarding matters of "faith and life." Yet it is still worthy of trust, albeit not a blind trust. Trust in that which is not God can never be uncritical.

Regarding inspiration, Froehlich disagrees with "modern doctrines of inspiration [that] are defensive reactions to the erosion of trust in the *literal* veracity of the historical narrative in the court of scientific historical research" (p. 25). In contrast, a dynamic, "liberating" understanding of inspiration, which does not *establish* authority, needs to be recovered from an earlier churchly process of spiritual reading; this can "free the texts from the strictures of their original historical settings . . . and open them for a new contextualization" (p. 27). Thus far, these are helpful reflections. But, in the process, he notes that church divines developed various spiritual interpretations, so that one could speak of the words of the Bible as having "more than one meaning." This opens up a new problem for the authority of the Bible. Because biblical authority is often tied to particular meanings of texts, the proliferation of legitimate readings will complicate how authority is understood. It will be important to explore just how such a perspective may link up with recent claims regarding textual indeterminacy, a matter I pursue, especially in chapter 4.

In his discussion of language, Froehlich rightly notes that language is "always imperfect, groping, vulnerable. . . . It participates in the openness of all human speech, which must be filled with specific meaning through specific human experience" (p. 44). While the Bible will never replace the need for personal faith experience, it "can help my personal experience find its language; it can interpret *me*" (p. 46). Biblical language is "an invitational language." It invites the reader to enter, and it has the capacity to make the reader feel at home (though not always comfortably so!). Because God "deigned to descend into the vulnerability of human speech and language . . . then it must be clear that God does not want to compel, to force, to ram any language down our throat." "The language of the Bible . . . is as tentative, as fragile, as experimental as any human speech" (p. 46). The exchange between experienced faith and the Bible is a rhythmic movement, but the Bible and its language remain the matrix to which we return again and again.

The integration of Scripture and experience "calls for and authorizes the bold new statement of faith which we must attempt time and again" (p. 49). In this analysis, Froehlich appeals to Lindbeck's formulation of intratextuality in which "the text so to speak . . . absorbs the world" (p. 51). Froehlich confesses a "considerable sympathy for a . . . narrative theology." He speaks of listening "in the story for the story. . . . This is what it would mean to hear God's Word in the Bible" (p. 59).

Once again, this implies that experience is finally drawn back into the Bible and its perspective, and such experience cannot stand over against the Bible and speak a "no" to one or another matter of which it speaks. But it must be said clearly that God is actively engaged in that worldly experience, and God may work in and through that experience in such a way as to bring a critical word to bear on the Bible. Difficult issues of discernment and criteria are quickly at hand, but we cannot in the face of those difficulties simply retreat into the narrative world of the Bible. For God is never simply "at home" in such a retreat.

1. *A Common Calling: The Witness of Our Reformation Churches in North America Today;* The Report of the Lutheran-Reformed Committee for Theological Conversations, 1988–1992, Keith F. Nickle and Timothy F. Lull, eds. (Minneapolis: Augsburg, 1993), 61-63.

2. See Peter Schaeffer, "The Emergence of the Concept 'Medieval' in Central European Humanism," *Sixteenth Century Journal* 7 (1973), 19-30.

3. See the two essays by W. Hartmann, "Modernus und antiquus: Zur Verbreitung und Bedeutung dieser Bezeichnungen in der wissenschaftlichen Literatur vom 9. bis zum 12. Jahrhundert," and Elisabeth Gössmann, "Antiqui und moderni im 12. Jahrhundert," in *Antiqui und Moderni: Traditionsbewusstsein und Fortschrittsbewusstsein im späten Mittelalter,* ed. Albert Zimmermann (Miscellanea Medievalia 9: Berlin: de Gruyter, 1973).

4. See Gerhard Ritter, *Via antiqua und via moderna auf den deutschen Universitäten des XV. Jahrhunderts* (Darmstadt: Wissenschaftliche Buchgesellschaft, 1963).

5. The quotation occurs in Toynbee's Gifford Lectures of 1952–53, which were published under the title *An Historian's Approach to Religion* (Oxford: Oxford University Press, 1956); see Part II, essay 11: "The Ascendancy of the Modern Western Civilization," p. 146. On the other uses of "postmodern," see *A Supplement to the Oxford Dictionary of the English Language,* ed. R. W. Burchfield, vol. 3 (Oxford: Clarendon, 1982), 698.

6. Quoted by Yves Congar, *Dialogue between Christians: Catholic Contributions to Ecumenism* (London and Dublin: Geoffrey Chapman, 1966), 41: "I remembered . . . a saying of Père Lacordaire which I have often repeated to myself since then: 'I have long thought that the most favourable time for sowing and planting are times of trouble and storms.'"

7. David Kelsey, *The Uses of Scripture in Recent Theology* (Philadelphia: Fortress Press, 1975), 97-98.

8. See Wilhelm Borth, *Die Luthersache (causa Lutheri) 1517–1524: Die Anfänge der Reformation als Frage von Politik und Recht* (Lübeck: Matthiesen-Verlag, 1970), 23-25.

9. These statements have appeared in several volumes in the series Lutherans and Catholics in Dialogue. See the list of the earlier volumes in *Justification by Faith,* ed. H. George Anderson, T. Austin Murphy, and Joseph A. Burgess (*Lutherans and Catholics in Dialogue* 7; Minneapolis: Augsburg, 1985), 316, note 1. Volume 8 was published under the title *The One Mediator, the Saints, and Mary*; Lutherans and Catholics in Dialogue, ed. H. George Anderson, J. Francis Stafford, Joseph A. Burgess. (Minneapolis: Augsburg, 1992). The most recent statement, *The Word of God: Scripture and Tradition,* was released in 1993.

10. See *Peter in the New Testament: A Collaborative Assessment by Protestant and Roman Catholic Scholars,* ed. Raymond E. Brown, Karl P. Donfried, and John Reumann (Minneapolis: Augsburg, and New York: Paulist Press, 1973), 7-22. The most recent official statement, "The Interpretation of the Bible in the Church," published by the Pontifical Biblical Commission in 1993 (the text is printed in full in *Origins* 23:29 [1994], 498-524), reflects this consensus clearly.

11. See *A Common Calling,* 25-30.

12. James I. Packer, *God Has Spoken* (Grand Rapids: Baker, 1988). The first edition was published in 1965 as a book for Anglicans. The author subsequently participated in the drafting of the 1978 statement and its 1982 sequel.

13. Jeffrey Stout, *The Flight from Authority: Religion, Morality, and the Quest for Autonomy* (Notre Dame: University of Notre Dame Press, 1981).

14. "Scriptural Authority and Theological Construction: The Limitations of Narrative Interpretation," in *Scriptural Authority and Narrative Interpretation,* ed. Garret Green (Philadelphia: Fortress Press, 1987), 42-58; here p. 53.

15. "Scriptural Authority," 42-43.

16. "Robin Scroggs, "The Bible as Foundational Document," *Interpretation* 49/1 (1995), 17-30; here 23, 19.

17. On this and the development of the general notion of authority, see the fascinating discussion in E. D. Watt, *Authority* (New York: St. Martin's Press, 1982).

18. This has been noted by the New Testament scholar, Ernst Käsemann, "Sentences of Holy Law," in his *New Testament Questions of Today,* trans. W. I. Montgomery (Philadelphia: Fortress Press, 1969), 66-81.

19. "The Authority of Scripture: A Catholic Perspective," in *Scripture in the Jewish and Christian Traditions: Authority, Interpretation, Relevance,* ed. Frederick E. Greenspahn (Nashville: Abingdon Press, 1982), 14-40; here p. 14.

20. On Lessing's graphic term, *der garstige breite Graben,* and its meaning, see Gordon Michalson, *Lessing's "Ugly Ditch": A Study of Theology and History* (University Park, Pa.: Pennsylvania State University Press, 1985).

21. See Augustin Bea, "*Deus auctor sacrae scripturae:* Herkunft und Bedeutung der Formel," *Angelicum* 20 (1943), 16-43.

22. See Bruce Vawter, "The Scholastic Synthesis: Instrumental Causality," chapter 3 in *Biblical Inspiration* (Theological Resources; Philadelphia: Westminster, 1972), 43-58.

23. Paul Achtemeier offers a thoughtful interpretation of this and related texts and of the broader issues in *The Inspiration of Scripture: Problems and Proposals* (Philadelphia: Westminster Press, 1980). On the notion of scriptural inspiration in the ancient world, I have found an older article by Johannes Leipoldt particularly helpful: "Frühgeschichte der Inspirationslehre," *Zeitschrift für die neutestamentliche Wissenschaft* 44 (1952-53), 118-45.

24. The notion of poetic inspiration is discussed in Plato's dialogue *Ion* 533-35; the criticism of poetic fiction is found in his *Republic* 376-78.

25. Philo, *Quis rerum divinarum heres sit,* 259.

26. On this story, see S. Jellicoe, *The Septuagint and Modern Study* (Oxford: Oxford University Press, 1968), 35-47. The *Letter of Aristeas* is translated by R. J. H. Shutt in *The Old Testament Pseudepigrapha,* ed. James H. Charlesworth, vol. 2 (New York: Doubleday, 1985), 7-34.

27. C. K. Barrett, *The New Testament Background: Selected Documents* (London: S.P.C.K., 1956), 211.

28. See Augustine, *Epistles* 28:2 and 71:3-4, in A Select Library of the Nicene and Post-Nicene Fathers of the Christian Church, ed. Philip Schaff; vol. 1, *The Confessions and Letters of St. Augustine* (repr., Grand Rapids: Eerdmans, 1974), 251 and 327-28.

29. Robert K. Johnston, *Evangelicals at an Impasse: Biblical Authority in Practice* (Atlanta: John Knox Press, 1979), 5.

30. On this doctrine in early Lutheran dogmatics, see Robert Preus, *The Inspiration of Scripture: A Study of the Seventeenth Century Lutheran Dogmaticians* (London: Oliver & Boyd, 1955); for the Reformed side, see Jack B. Rogers, *Scripture in the Westminster Confession: A Problem of Historical Interpretation for American Presbyterians* (Kampen: J. H. Kok, 1966); and Jack B. Rogers and Donald K. McKim, *The Authority and Interpretation of the Bible: An Historical Approach* (San Francisco: Harper & Row, 1979), chapter 3: "Concern for Literary Form."

31. See below, note 117.

32. "On Lying," and "To Consentius: Against Lying," trans. H. Browne in A Select Library of the Nicene and Post-Nicene Fathers of the Christian Church, ed. Philip Schaff; vol. 3, *St. Augustine: On the Holy Trinity; Doctrinal Treatises; Moral Treatises* (repr., Grand Rapids: Eerdmans, 1974), 457-500.

33. See Marinus M. Woesthuis, "'Nunc ad historiam revertamur': History and Preaching in Helinand of Froidmont," *Sacris Eruditi* 34 (1994), 313-33; here pp. 320-23.

34. See Enrique Nardoni, "Origen's Concept of Biblical Inspiration," *The Second Century* 4/1 (1984), 9-23.

35. Origen, *On First Principles* 3.1; see my translation in *Biblical Interpretation in the Early Church* (Sources of Early Christian Thought; Philadelphia: Fortress Press, 1984), 63.

36. On the history of the fourfold sense, see my article, "Johannes Trithemius on the Fourfold Sense of Scripture: The *Tractatus de Inuestigatione Sacrae Scripturae* (1486)," in *Biblical Interpretation in the Era of the Reformation: Essays Presented to David C. Steinmetz in Honor of His Sixtieth Birthday,* Richard A. Muller and John L. Thompson, eds. (Grand Rapids: Eerdmans, 1996), 23-60; here pp. 38-55.

37. Augustine's thoughts on these matters are most fully discussed in his hermeneutical treatise, *Saint Augustine: On Christian Doctrine,* trans. D. W. Robertson (The Library of Liberal Arts; New York: Macmillan, 1987).

38. "The Old Testament contains the Law, the Prophets, and the Hagiographers; the New contains the Gospel, the Apostles, and the Fathers," *The Didascalicon of Hugh of Saint Victor. A Medieval Guide to the Arts,* trans. Jerome Taylor (Columbia Records of Civilization; New York and London: Columbia University Press, 1961), 4.2, p. 103.

39. "The Will to Choose or Reject: Continuing Our Critical Work," in *Feminist Interpretation of the Bible,* ed. Letty M. Russell (Philadelphia: Westminster Press, 1985), 114. Schüssler Fiorenza's major contribution, *In Memory of Her,* was published by Crossroad in 1983.

40. See Appendix I: "History of the Word *Kanon*," in Bruce M. Metzger, *The Canon of the New Testament: Its Origin, Development, and Significance* (Oxford: Clarendon, 1987), 289-93.

41. Eusebius, *Church History* 7.25. On Eusebius's New Testament canon, see Metzger, *The Canon of the New Testament,* 202-96.

42. See Bart D. Ehrman, "The Text of Mark in the Hands of the Orthodox," in *Biblical Hermeneutics in Historical Perspective: Studies in Honor of Karlfried Froehlich on His Sixtieth Birthday,* ed. M. S. Burrows and P. Rorem (Grand Rapids: Eerdmans, 1991), 19-31.

43. Kelsey, *The Uses of Scripture,* esp. 100-108.

44. Metzger, *The Canon of the New Testament,* 282-88.

45. See Paul R. Noble, *The Canonical Approach: A Critical Reconstruction of the Hermeneutics of Brevard Childs* (Biblical Interpretation Series 16; Leiden: Brill, 1995). He has a good, brief characterization also in "The Interpretation of the Bible in the Church," *Origins* 23:29 (1994), 504-5.

46. See Harry Gamble, *The New Testament Canon: Its Making and Meaning* (Guides to Biblical Scholarship; Philadelphia: Fortress Press, 1985), 75.

47. Everett R. Kalin, "The Inspired Community: A Glance at Canon History," *Concordia Theological Monthly* 42 (1971), 541-49.

48. Carl Braaten seems to allow a positive answer when he makes a distinction between revelation and salvation: "There are many media of revelation; only one medium of final salvation, Jesus Christ himself." "Interreligious Dialogue in the Pluralistic Situation," *Dialog* 33:4 (1994), 296-97.

49. *De doctrina christiana,* 1.36.40; see *Saint Augustine: On Christian Doctrine,* trans. D. W. Robertson (The Library of Liberal Arts, 80; Indianapolis: Bobbs-Merrill, 1958), 30.

50. Ibid., 1.39.43; p. 32.

51. Ibid., 7.9.13f.; see *Saint Augustine: Confessions,* trans. R. S. Pine-Coffin (Baltimore: Penguin, 1961), 144-45.

52. See Robert Preus, *The Inspiration of Scripture: A Study of the Seventeenth Century Lutheran Dogmaticians* (London: Oliver & Boyd, 1955).

53. See John Baillie's Bampton Lectures of 1954, published as *The Idea of Revelation in Recent Thought* (New York: Columbia University Press, 1956), and Avery Dulles, *Models of Revelation,* 2d ed. (Maryknoll, N.Y.: Orbis, 1992).

54. F. Gerald Downing, *Has Christianity a Revelation?* (Philadelphia: Westminster Press, 1964).

55. "Sermon on Exodus, Chapter 9, Dec. 26, 1524"; WA 16, 143:34—144:13-21.33.

56. See Laurent Volken, *Visions, Revelations, and the Church,* trans. E. Gallagher (New York: P. J. Kenedy and Sons, 1963).

57. Thomas discussed the subject in his treatise on special charisms under the rubric of prophecy, *Summa theologiae* 2/2, questions 171-178.

58. *Corpus Iuris Canonici: Decretum Gratiani,* ed. Emil Friedberg (Leipzig: B. Tauchnitz, 1879), Part 2, Causa 19, Question 2; vol. 1, col. 840. Here, the question whether a person desiring to enter a monastic vocation must be accepted even against the will of his bishop, is solved by a citation from a letter of Pope Urban II (d. 1099): "There are two laws, a public and a private one. . . . The private law is written on the heart by instigation of the Holy Spirit as the Apostle writes of some 'who have the law of God written in their hearts' (Rom. 2:15), and elsewhere: 'when the gentiles, who do not have the law, do by nature those things that are of the law, they are a law to themselves' (Rom. 2:14). If one of these restrains his people in a parish under the bishop and lives a worldly life, but then under the inspiration of the Holy Spirit wants to find his salvation in a monastery or house of regular canons, there is no reason that he should be restrained by the public law since he is guided by the private law. For the private law is worthier than the public. The Spirit of God is law, and those who are led by the Spirit of God are led by the law of God. Who is worthy to resist the Holy Spirit? Therefore, whoever is led by this Spirit may go freely by our authority, even against the will of his bishop. For the law is not made for the righteous person, and where the Spirit of the Lord is, there is freedom, and if you are led by the Spirit, you are not under the law."

59. See Paschal Boland, O.S.B., *The Concept of Discretio Spirituum in John Gerson's "De Probatione Spirituum and De Distinctione Verarum Visionum a Falsis* (The Catholic University of America Studies in Sacred Theology, 2d ser., no. 112; Washington, D.C.: Catholic University of America Press, 1959).

60. "[W]e must hold firmly to the conviction that God gives no one his Spirit or grace except through or with the external Word which comes before. Thus we shall be protected from the enthusiasts. . . . The papacy, too, is nothing but enthusiasm, for the pope boasts that 'all laws are in the shrine of his heart,' and he claims that whatever he decides and commands in his churches is spirit and law. . . ." Smalcald Articles, Article 8, in *The Book of Concord,* ed. T. G. Tappert (Philadelpha: Fortress Press, 1959), 312.

61. "Das 16. Kapitel Sankt Johannes gepredigt und ausgelegt," WA 46, 62:12-15; cf. Luther's Works, 24: 367.

62. "Sermon on John 17:4-6; August 29, 1538," WA 28, 101:24-28.

63. See *The Cosmotheandric Experience: Emerging Religious Consciousness* (Maryknoll, N.Y.: Orbis, 1993); also *The Trinity and the Religious Experience of Man: Icon-Person-Mystery* (New York: Orbis, 1973) and *The Unknown Christ of Hinduism: Towards an Ecumenical Christophany,* rev. ed. (Maryknoll, N.Y.: Orbis, 1981).

64. See Bruce Metzger, *The Canon of the New Testament* (above, note 40), 275-82.

65. See chapter 9, "Jesus the Word," in Oscar Cullmann, *The Christology of the New Testament,* rev. ed. (Philadelphia: Westminster, 1963), 249-69.

66. See Athanasius's treatise, "On the Incarnation of the Word," in *Christology of the Later Fathers,* ed. E. R. Hardy (Library of Christian Classics 3; Philadelphia: Westminster, 1954), 55-110; the quotation here is from p. 107.

67. Ibid., 373.

68. See my essay, "The Libri Carolini and the Lessons of the Iconoclastic Controversy," in *The One Mediator, the Saints, and Mary*; Lutherans and Catholics in Dialogue 8, ed. H. George Anderson, J. Francis Stafford, and Joseph A. Burgess (Minneapolis: Augsburg, 1992), 193-208; 374-76.

69. See *Liturgy and Hymns,* ed. U. S. Leupold (Luther's Works 53; Philadelphia: Fortress Press, 1965), 241.

70. *The Myth of God Incarnate,* ed. John Hick (London: SCM, 1977).

71. See the "Preface to the Reissue," xi-xiv.
72. Frances Young, "Two Roots or a Tangled Mess?" 87-121; see also her introductory essay, "A Cloud of Witnesses," 13-47.
73. On the role of experience in modern theological culture, see Gerhard Ebeling's thoughtful article, "Schrift und Erfahrung als Quelle theologischer Aussagen," *Zeitschrift für Theologie und Kirche* 75 (1978), 99-116.
74. See Eugen Drewermann, *Tiefenpsychologie und Exegese,* vol. 1 (Olten: Walter-Verlag, 1984), section 1,1: "Vom religiösen Irrweg der historisch-kritischen Methode—eine Standortbestimmung," 23-28; here p. 25.
75. *Tiefenpsychologie und Exegese,* vol. 2 (Olten: Walter-Verlag, 1985), Einführung: "Von vier Gefahren der Theologie—der Exegese aber im besonderen. 1. Das erfahrungslose Sprechen von fremden Erfahrungen oder: Das Brotgelehrtentum," 13-18.
76. Ibid., 66-72 and 773f.
77. Drewermann has made this point in several autobiographical reflections, especially in *Was ich denke* (Munich: Goldmann, 1994), 60-44; and *Worum es eigentlich geht: Protokoll einer Verurteilung* (Munich: Kösel, 2d ed., 1992), 290-92. It is also highlighted in a contribution by a colleague sympathetic to his cause, Peter Eicher; ibid., pp. 488-90. The last-mentioned publication presents a voluminous documentation of the events surrounding the official proceedings against Drewermann from his point of view.
78. Mary Daly, *The Church and the Second Sex* (New York: Harper & Row, 1968; Boston: Beacon, 1985); *Beyond God the Father: Toward a Philosophy of Women's Liberation* (Boston: Beacon, 1973; 1985).
79. See her essay, "Authority and the Challenge of Feminist Interpretation," in *The Feminist Interpretation of the Bible,* ed. Letty M. Russell (Philadelphia: Westminster, 1985), 136-46.
80. Elisabeth Schüssler Fiorenza, "The Will to Choose or Reject: Continuing Our Critical Work," in *The Feminist Interpretation of the Bible,* 128.

81. Rosemary Radford Ruether, "Feminist Interpretation: A Method of Correlation," in *The Feminist Interpretation of the Bible*, 111. See also her *Womenguides: Readings Toward a Feminist Theology* (Boston: Beacon Press, 1985), and *Women-Church: Theology and Practice of Feminist Liturgical Communities* (San Francisco: Harper & Row, 1985; 1988).

82. See Luba Eleen, *The Illustration of the Pauline Epistles in French and English Bibles of the Twelfth and Thirteenth Centuries* (Oxford: Clarendon, 1982), esp. chapter 3.

83. English translations in the series *Ancient Christian Writers*, vol. 9; *The Fathers of the Church*, vol. 59; and in *Augustine: Earlier Writings*, ed. J. H. S. Burleigh (Library of Christian Classics 6; Philadelphia: Westminster, 1953), 69-101.

84. George A. Lindbeck, *The Nature of Doctrine: Religion and Theology in a Post-Liberal Age* (Philadelphia: Westminster, 1984), esp. chapter 1.

85. Ibid., 33.

86. Oscar Cullmann, *The Earliest Christian Confessions* (London: Lutterworth, 1949), chapter 3.

87. See Paul F. Palmer, *Sacraments and Worship* (Sources of Christian Theology 1; Westminster, Md.: Newman, 1955), 29f.

88. *Christliches Gesangbuch oder Sammlung evangelischer Kernlieder und geistlicher Gesänge*, ed. H. Fröhlich (Dresden: Selbstverlag des Herausgebers, 1872).

89. *Lutheran Book of Worship*, Hymn 48, stanza 2: "God's Son to whom the heavens bow / Cradled by a virgin now, / We listen for your infant voice / While angels in your heav'n rejoice. Hallelujah!" For the original German text and a more precise English translation, see above, note 69.

90. They are *LBW* Hymn 374, "We all believe in one true God" (creed), and 79, "To Jordan came the Christ, our Lord" (baptism).

91. Luther started the trend with his two catechisms of 1529, the Small and the Large Catechism, which form part of the Lutheran confessional writings. On early Reformed catechisms,

see Thomas F. Torrance, *The School of Faith: The Catechisms of the Reformed Church* (London: C. Clarke, 1959).

92. He did this at the very beginning of his *Church Dogmatics,* where he was formulating the "thesis" of paragraph 1: *Church Dogmatics,* 1/1, The Doctrine of the Word of God (Edinburgh: T. & T. Clark, 1975), 3-4.

93. See the section on the development of the exegetical "question" in Beryl Smalley's book, *The Study of the Bible in the Middle Ages* (Oxford: Basil Blackwell, 1952; 3d ed., 1993), 66-82.

94. Augustine, *On Christian Doctrine* (see above, note 37), Prologue, section 4, p. 4.

95. Hugh of St. Victor, "De tribus maximis circumstantiis," ed. Greene, *Speculum* 18 (1943), 489:27-41.

96. "There I began to understand that the righteousness of God is that by which the righteous lives by a gift of God, namely by faith. . . . Here I felt that I was altogether born again and had entered paradise itself through open gates. There a totally other face of the entire Scripture showed itself to me. Thereupon I ran through the Scriptures from memory. I also found in other terms an analogy. . . ." From "Preface to the Latin Writings, 1545," in *Martin Luther: Selections from His Writings,* ed. John Dillenberger (Anchor Books; Garden City, N.Y.: Doubleday, 1961), 11.

97. See the report by Marlise Simons, "Brother Roger Calls, and 110,000 Youths Respond," *The New York Times,* international ed., Monday, January 2, 1995, p. 4.

98. Latourette wrote the classic missionary *History of the Expansion of Christianity* in seven volumes. Three volumes are devoted to the period between 1800 and 1914: vol. 4: *The Great Century;* vol. 5: *The Great Century in the Americas, Australasia and Africa;* vol. 6: *The Great Century in Northern Africa and Asia.*

99. Gerhard Ebeling, "Schrift und Erfahrung als Quelle theologischer Aussagen," *Zeitschrift für Theologie und Kirche* 75 (1978), 99-116.

100. Ibid., 108.

101. "Sermon on 1 Cor. 15:1-8, August 1532," WA 36, 506:18-33; cf. Luther's Works, 28:81.

102. Gerhard Ebeling, "Hermeneutik zwischen der Macht des Gotteswortes und seiner Entmachtung in der Moderne," *Zeitschrift für Theologie und Kirche* 91 (1994), 80-96.

103. "First Psalms Commentary, 1513-1516," on Ps. 68, WA 3, 397:9-11; cf. Luther's Works, 10: 332.

104. Lindbeck, *The Nature of Doctrine,* 118.

105. Commentary on Galatians (1535), on Gal. 2:14, WA 40/1, 207:1-4; cf. Luther's Works, 26:115. See also Eric W. Gritsch, *Martin—God's Court Jester: Luther in Retrospect* (Philadelphia: Fortress Press, 1983), 171f.

106. "Justification by Faith: Common Statement," par. 88-93, in *Justification by Faith,* ed. H. G. Anderson, T. A. Murphy, and Joseph A. Burgess (Lutherans and Catholics in Dialogue 7; Minneapolis: Augsburg, 1985), 47-48.

107. "Church Postill on Matt. 2:1-12," WA 10/1, 17:7-13; cf. Luther's Works, 35:123.

108. Ibid., 627:1-9.

109. Ibid., 625:19—626:18.

110. See Albert B. Lord, *The Singer of Tales* (New York: Atheneum, 1968), and its sequel, *The Singer Resumes the Tale,* ed. Mary Louise Lord (Ithaca, N.Y.: Cornell University Press, 1995). The author seeks to find clues for the interpretation of Homer in the oral art of modern-day epic singers in South Slavic languages.

111. *Phaedrus* 274c-275b, in *The Collected Dialogues of Plato,* ed. Edith Hamilton and Huntington Cairns (Bollingen Series 71; Princeton University Press, 1961), 520.

112. See "The Fragments of Papias," in The Apostolic Fathers: A New Translation and Commentary, ed. Robert M. Grant, vol. 5: *Polycarp, Martyrdom of Polycarp, Fragments of Papias,* trans. William R. Schoedel (London: Thomas Nelson & Sons, 1967), 101.

113. *Eclogae propheticae* 27:1 (Die griechischen christlichen Schriftsteller der ersten drei Jahrhunderte, 17; *Clemens von Alexandrien:*

Excerpta und Eclogae propheticae, ed. O. Stählin (Leipzig: Hinrich, 1909), 144:26.

114. "Concerning Idolatry" 23:5 (The Ante-Nicene Fathers, 3; Grand Rapids: Eerdmans, 1989), 75.

115. Irenaeus's argument is contained in the five books of his "The Refutation and Overthrow of the Knowledge Falsely So-Called" ("Against Heresies"); it is summarized in 3.1-2 (see *Early Christian Fathers,* trans. and ed. Cyril C. Richardson; Library of Christian Classics 1 [Philadelphia: Westminster Press, 1953], 370f.).

116. See *Bilanz der Theologie im 20. Jahrhundert: Bahnbrechende Theologen,* ed. Herbert Vorgrimler (Freiburg: Herder, 1970), 101.

117. On Martin Luther's understanding of this verse and the exegetical tradition, see Kenneth Hagen, "*Omnis homo mendax:* Luther on Psalm 116," in *Biblical Interpretation in the Era of the Reformation: Essays Presented to David C. Steinmetz in Honor of His Sixtieth Birthday,* Richard A. Muller and John L. Thompson, eds. (Grand Rapids: Eerdmans, 1996), 85-102.

118. The concept of the Bible as a "classic" is the basis on which Roman Catholic scholar David Tracy argued for a universal form of biblical authority in a pluralistic culture. See his book, *The Analogical Imagination: Christian Theology and the Culture of Pluralism* (New York: Crossroads, 1981).

119. Among Frei's important publications are *The Eclipse of Biblical Narrative* (New Haven: Yale University Press, 1974) and several essays in the volume, *Theology and Narrative: Selected Essays,* ed. George Hunsinger and William Placher (New York: Oxford University Press, 1993). A "selected bibliography of works by and about Hans Frei" is included in the volume *Scriptural Authority and Narrative Interpretation,* ed. G. Green (Philadelphia: Fortress Press, 1987), 199-201.

120. "Exegetical Storytelling: Liberation of the Traditions from the Text," in *The Bible and the Politics of Exegesis. Essays in Honor of Norman K. Gottwald on His Sixty-Fifth Birthday,* ed. David Jobling, Peggy L. Day, and Gerald T. Sheppard (Cleveland: Pilgrim, 1991), 83-93.

121. Parallel instances are, e.g., Isa 9:7; Ps 107:20; Isa 55:10-11; *Wis.* 18:15.

122. Long Text, chapter 51, in *Julian of Norwich: Showings,* trans. E. Colledge and J. Walsh (Classics of Western Spirituality; New York: Paulist Press, 1978), 267-69.

123. *Lutheran Book of Worship,* Hymn 299, stanza 5; cf. Luther's Works, 53: *Liturgy and Hymns* (Philadelphia: Fortress Press, 1965), 217-20.

PART II

By
Terence E. Fretheim

CHAPTER 4

The Bible as Word of God
in a Postmodern Age

THE QUESTION OF BIBLICAL AUTHORITY IS MUCH IN THE AIR IN THESE postmodern days. The word "crisis" often appears in the discussion. While this question is especially lively among those who hold the Bible dear, the dialogue spills out into the larger culture. The use of the Bible in the culture wars catches up "outsiders" in the conversation or, at the least, it makes many such people nervous. It is generally recognized that Christians do not speak with one voice about this matter, but it is not easy to sort out those voices.

I do not pretend to bring order to this discussion; in some ways the issues presented may complicate matters. Nor is this an effort to speak in any comprehensive way about the authority of the Bible. Rather, my concern is to raise up certain factors in current biblical interpretation that need to be taken into account in speaking about biblical authority. My assumption throughout is that the present crisis has less to do with the authority of the Bible as such and more with the authority of differing *interpretations* of certain biblical texts and themes, and how those differences are to be adjudicated.

In this chapter, I approach the topic in more general terms, with issues presented by culture, church, and academy. In chapters 5 and 6 I focus on the biblical portrayal of God and the often facile assumption that the Bible always speaks the truth about God. When the Bible speaks of God, is it always trustworthy or coherent or true to human experience?

The issue of the authority of the Bible is often considered a modern problem. But it is better said that the contemporary world has intensified what has long been a problem for the Bible. Maurice Wiles puts it this way: "There has never been a golden age when Scripture functioned in an unproblematic manner in the life of the church. There have always been attendant difficulties."[1] One need only mention the second-century figure Marcion, who cut out the Old Testament and much of the New, or the Alexandrian school, which, when faced with troubling texts (e.g., regarding the passibility of God), appealed to an allegorical hermeneutic. The issue is more complex and intense today, however, not least because problems of authority for previous generations have not often been resolved, and the modern world has added its own issues. I can understand why fundamentalistic folk often ignore the problems and affirm the Bible's absolute authority with no qualifications whatsoever. But the church and its Bible are not well served by hiding from the very real problems the Bible presents for those who claim it to be the Word of God.

As a way of beginning, let me suggest a preliminary understanding of the Bible as Word of God: the Bible's unique capacity to mediate God's word of judgment and grace, which can effect life and salvation for individuals and communities. While the focus of the Bible's authority is this formational role, the Scripture also has informational capacities. It delineates what the Christian faith essentially was and still properly is, it identifies what the basic shape for Christian life in the world was and still properly is, and, more generally, it tells the truth about the world, though not the whole truth, certainly.

This claim for biblical authority is derivative; it follows from the belief that the God of the Bible is Lord. Without that confession, the Bible is a book like many other books. The Bible's authority will only be acknowledged if, through its use, people see that it speaks to their needs of life, well-being, and the flourishing of their communities in the world. The question of biblical authority, then, is most basically an inside, churchly conversation; but this conversation will spill out into the larger culture and affect the church's witness, positively or negatively.

The crisis of authority in our time may be ordered in terms of three overlapping spheres: the culture more generally, the churches, and the academy. We must not be uncritical of the developments outlined here, but they are realities with which we must come to terms in thinking of biblical authority.

1. *The culture.* One characteristic of our current context is that people, both within and without the church, are suspicious of authority. This includes the authority claimed by leaders in church and society or anyone's claims to have a corner on the truth. Nothing is tied down anymore; everything is up for grabs. Everyone, it seems, has a right to her or his own opinion. Christians may have whatever views about the Bible they like, of course, but they had best not try to impose them on others.

Besides egalitarian commitments that contribute to this mentality, people have learned that it is right to be suspicious; too many monsters have been let loose in the world in the name of authority, including biblical authority. And so, all claims for authority have to be re-thought, and how best to do that is one issue that animates the current discussion. But one way that will not work is to begin with a universal claim or an appeal to special privilege. In such a situation, the Bible no longer starts with any advantage; special appeals to inspiration or revelation or the Word of God count for little. The Bible will have to take its place alongside other possible authorities and make its own way. If we were to think in terms of a marathon, the Bible has the same starting place as any other book. If it is going to win the race, it will have to prove its value for life and well-being in the heat of the day. We might lament this situation, but it is real, and a simple repetition of the old verities will not cut it anymore.

An important factor in this situation is religious pluralism; the Bible's authority is contested by other claims to authority among our increasingly diverse neighbors. Our once dominant Christian culture is disappearing; alternate religious voices are heard in the land and often heeded. To use another image, the Bible has to compete in a marketplace of authorities, and a buyer's market prevails, where universal claims, overwrought promises, and shrill rhetoric are greeted with increasing incredulity and suspicion. Christians are often not well prepared to live with or adjudicate among competing authorities, and, with their Bible in their hands, they are often reduced either to silence or screaming. In either case, the status of the Bible is diminished still further.

Another factor in our current situation is a sharply individualistic orientation, with the loss of a sense of an overarching community that has a universalizable story. If, as we shall see, the Bible's authority is closely tied to the way in which it functions within community, and if people do not experience genuine community, the place of the Bible will suffer. The Bible tends to be viewed more in isolation, say, in terms of its support for an individual viewpoint. But if the Bible does not support, or perhaps subverts, an individual's likes and dislikes, especially those causes most dear, then of what earthly use is it? From another angle, our situation is also characterized by the emergence of numerous subcommunities, each of which has its own story and ideology. If the Bible claims to have a story that applies to everyone, but it does not fit with the particular story of such a community, then its claim is suspect. Or, if a subcommunity, with its particular ideology, claims the Bible to be its authority, other communities may well dismiss the Bible because of its link to that ideology.

A further factor is the loss of a sense of transcendence. This is an especially crucial matter and undergirds the decision to devote the next two chapters to issues of God and Bible. If the God whom the church presents to the world is unattractive and God is rejected, then the rejection of the Bible follows as a matter of course. Or, if certain biblical images for God become problematic, even within the church, then God may be diminished in people's eyes, and that in turn will diminish biblical authority.

2. *The churches.* Suspicions about the Bible are also embedded within the churches themselves. The authority of the Bible is no longer a given among many Christian folk, at least in any traditional sense. Certainly the intrusion of the above-noted cultural realities into the life of the congregations is a factor, as is an unfamiliarity with the Bible and its often strange vocabulary. The Bible more and more needs to be explained, even to persons long associated with the church. When you do not get it, it is easy to ignore it or dismiss it. The fact that for years in

the churches a Bible piety has not been matched by a Bible literacy is coming home to roost.

Another key factor: Christians have often alienated people from the Bible by the way in which they have used it. Because authority is closely tied to use, this is a powerful reality. Christians who disagree about a whole host of matters, from homosexuality to the place of women in the church, often use the Bible in highly polemical ways, more as a bludgeon or an Uzi than as a source of life. The not uncommon reaction is: "If the Bible causes such division, violence, and vituperative behavior, I don't need it." Ironically, the authority of the Bible is thereby diminished by those who hold it most dear. We should admit that church people are as responsible as any for the hard times on which the Bible has fallen and the suspicion with which it is viewed. Given the continued use of the Bible in the culture wars, it is probably going to get worse for the Bible, not better. Another way to put the matter: such a polemical use of the Bible has the effect of blunting God's mission in the world. Causes polemically pursued with Bible in hand push off to the edges that central biblical word of what God has done for the world in Jesus Christ.

In the churches the Bible's authority is often tied to specific *interpretations* of certain texts. When disagreements arise among Christians regarding such interpretations, the fundamental issue often is not the authority of the Bible as such, though the rhetoric sometimes bends that way, but the way in which certain texts are to be interpreted and the authority of the resultant interpretation. Some interpretations seem to be given an authority approximating that of the Bible itself; if they are challenged, then the very authority of the Bible is thought to be called into question. The lack of an agreed-upon way of adjudicating among differing interpretations of texts severely complicates moves toward resolving such issues. At the least, we might hope that no interpretation would be thought to stand outside the need for evaluation, lest the interpretation be elevated to a status comparable to the biblical text itself.

These various developments lead me to ask several questions: Do we need a high view of the authority of the Bible to be effectively about God's purposes in the world? Is the church wasting its time and energy being defensive about the Bible or engaging in debates about its authority? We know well that groups who hold the Bible in highest esteem—say, Jehovah's Witnesses—are not thereby guaranteed insight into the truth about God or made more effective in furthering God's mission. Can, in fact, one's views about the Bible get in the way of mission? The Word of God we are to bring to the world is not a word about the Bible and its authority. Any view of the Bible must be of such a nature that it does not detract from the hearing of the gospel. Might it be that, for the sake of mission, God himself is behind the diminishment of the status of the Bible? Should we, perhaps, rejoice in what has happened to the Bible's authority? Should we not just proceed to preach and teach from biblical texts and let whatever esteem the Bible may gain grow out of that encounter? Perhaps our basic motto ought to be: Use the Bible or lose it. Perhaps David Clines is correct: "When a fearsome dogma has been overpowered and shorn of its authority, we take to it more kindly and are attracted by its defenselessness . . . and even fall to wondering whether there was not perhaps some quality in it that might account for its having become a dogma in the first place."[2] This is a kind of theology of the cross or incarnational approach to the Bible; the Bible exemplifies its power in and through weakness. We have this treasure in earthen vessels. Would not such an approach be more consistent with some of our most basic theological instincts? Would not this mean that a proper understanding of biblical authority focuses on its dialogical character? The Bible exercises its authority in and through its genuine engagement with the lives of people.

3. *The academy*. Recent developments from within the biblical disciplines, influenced by ways of knowing in other fields, have complicated the issue of authority. Walter Brueggemann speaks of a shift away from a centered biblical consensus marked by three interrelated developments.[3]

- The voice of new interpreters formerly kept at the margins of the academy and churchly scholarship, especially women and Third World scholars. The old ways of knowing that are

Euro-American, white, and male have become deeply suspect as ideologically driven, and command less and less respect.

- Newer methods, such as the new literary criticism, have broken away from historical models and from the assumptions of scholarly objectivity.

- A shift away from a focus on the mighty acts of God or the covenant to neglected texts and themes related to wisdom, creation, or those in which women or the oppressed play a special role.

Let me focus on how new ways of reading the Bible have complicated issues of authority. Once again, this is no uniquely modern problem; every generation has had its new ways of reading. One thinks of allegorical approaches, Reformation emphases, and historical methods. Historical criticism in particular sparked much discussion about matters of authority, not least because it was a response to ecclesiastical authoritarianism. But the new literary criticism has raised these issues even more sharply, not least because historical criticism largely left the theological issues unengaged or assumed the classical theological consensus; this is not the case with new literary approaches.

One such expression is reader-response criticism, where the focus has shifted from authors of texts to readers of texts. "Rather than seeing 'meaning' as a property inherent in the texts themselves, whether put there by the author (as in historical criticism) or intrinsic to the structure of the texts (as in rhetorical criticism), reader-response criticism regards meaning as coming into being at the meeting point of text and reader—or, in a more extreme form, as created by readers in the act of reading."[4]

Such an approach (among others) has brought a new level of self-awareness as to how our personal perspectives affect our readings of the Bible, and how sheer objectivity in reading is a mirage. As is increasingly seen to be the case, even in the sciences, the interests of the knower intrude powerfully into the knowing process. Any simple distinction between "what the text meant" and "what the text means" has been shown to be wrongheaded, indeed arrogant. Readers have preunderstandings and predispositions—personal, social, cultural, religious—that affect what is known, indeed help constitute it; it makes a difference to Bible reading whether you are male or female, black or white, upper class or lower class. Indeed, the persistence of cultural change ensures that readings of the Bible will be always on the move. The more complex our cultures, our churches, and our academies become, the more we will be faced with differing readings of biblical texts.

Even more, such readings are not innocent; they are always to some degree ideologically driven. Human sinfulness, let alone finitude, inhibits, indeed undermines, our ability to read the Bible in disinterested ways. For example, if we are the ones in power in society or church, our readings of the Bible will tend to hold sway. All too often the prevailing biblical readings correspond to the theology of the power brokers in the church; other readings will be considered heretical, inappropriate methodologically, or silly. In such hands, the Bible is used in the service of the prevailing ideology; it is turned into a club to wield social, political, and ecclesiastical control. Given this reality of power over centuries of interpretation, even with occasional contrary voices, many Bible readers are suspicious of univocal readings or readings that seek to make everything consistent and coherent. And rightly so.

Differing emphases exist in reader-response criticism, and one could engage in various debates about this and that; at this point, I lift up a few basic considerations about the indeterminacy of meaning. Long-established approaches to the Bible have assumed a determinate meaning, an original or true or intended meaning of the text. But this is now sharply called into question in view of the role that readers, with their differing social locations and interests, play in the making of meaning. Generally, from this perspective, meanings are not contained within the text, as if waiting to be unearthed; they are generated in readerly conversation with that text. For David Clines: "There is no one authentic meaning [of any biblical text] which we must all try to discover."[5] Nor, I would add, is the interpreter to think that the definitive meaning of any text has been determined, so that one might conceivably conclude: we have to date discovered the proper meaning of, say, 34% of the biblical texts. No meaning ought ever be considered *the* meaning or a final meaning of a text. Reading is a dialogical process in which the contribution of both text and reader is important for meaning; "what readers do to a text is just as constitutive of meaning as what the text does to the readers."[6] While one might quarrel over the "just as," meaning changes over time not only for different readers, but for the same reader, for readers are different persons every time they read the text. Generally, I would say that multiple meanings arise over time "in the conversation between the text and the reader with the world behind the text informing that conversation."[7] Meanings of texts, then, will always be to some degree open-ended; they are not fixed and stable. But, importantly, both text and reader must be held accountable for the effects these ever-changing readings may have on other people. Ethical responsibility in reading will be a theme in the pages to follow.

In addition, Christians must speak of a third party at work in this dialogical process, namely, God the Holy Spirit, whose engagement in the interaction of reader and text also contributes to the production of meaning. The differing spiritual experiences and sensitivities of readers will affect the nature of this interaction. Meanings emerge, then, from within this text/reader/God conversational encounter. Once again, I stress the language of conversation and dialogue.

It is important to remember that to reduce the text to a single meaning fails to take certain *historical* realities into account. Many Old Testament texts in their present form are composite in character; they are the end result of centuries of revision and redaction at the hands of numerous ancient interpreters, all of whom are anonymous. In other words, numerous readings of the tradition over time now reside *within the text*. So the texts themselves do not speak with one voice; they have many layered meanings, and it is usually impossible to sort them out. To speak of an original or intended meaning is simply not being true to the historical character of the text. The diversity of meanings we may uncover in our contemporary readings may well often correspond to the inner-biblical diversity of meanings.

Moreover, in thinking about the intention of the transmitters of texts, it may be that they often had rather amorphous meanings in mind, which cannot be captured in a "what it meant." For example, they may have wanted to draw readers into the story being told, or to teach them the Word of God, or to spark their imagination regarding faith and life, or to evoke a range of memories or feelings. Indeed, all or none of these possibilities may have come into play, so that, in either case, the proper *historical* comment is to say that there were *no* original or intended meanings of specific texts, or at most an interest in generating meanings.

But do no constraints on meaning possibilities exist? Are there as many meanings as there are readers? At least two limiting factors should be considered. The upshot: the text cannot mean anything just because it can mean many things.

1. The text itself. The never-changing words on the page provide constraints; distinctive textual features (e.g., prose or poetry) influence readings in certain directions and not in others. Moreover, the text was shaped by certain realities in the culture within which it was produced, and these need to be taken into account, though they are usually elusive and ambiguous as to their import. Texts do shape readers; readers are not in full control of meanings nor do they create them out of whole cloth. Adele Berlin puts it this way: "[J]ust as no reading is free of input from the reader, so no reading is free of input from the text."[8]

Yet, the text is not as stable as one might think. A text may include gaps, silences, polysemic words, or grammatical ambiguities—all of which can affect interpretation greatly. For example, how does one translate the ambiguous grammar of Gen 1:1-3 or the Shema (Deut 6:4)? The meanings of these texts, indeed of Deuteronomy 6 and Genesis 1 and the larger contexts of which they are a part, are shaped by the translation. More generally, of course, we remember that the meanings of texts are not self-evident in the words on the page, and so preaching, teaching, and scholarly work are deemed necessary. We seek to interpret the text, not simply to read it. So, for all of its stability, the text can be a source of instability. Texts never stay still for readers. The proliferation of modern Bible translations is reflective of this reality.

2. Another constraining factor on meaning possibilities is that both text and reader reside within communities.

As for *texts,* they are not autonomous. As Peter Miscall puts it, "No text is an island."[9] Texts exist only in a web of community beliefs about the Bible or about particular texts and their meaning; these realities shape our reading before we even pick up the text.[10] For example, no biblically educated person can read a text such as Psalm 23 without bringing to that reading some sense of its meaning and import. A look at Psalm 23 in some naked form, if you will, is no longer possible. At the same time, communities can change and accumulate more intense life experiences, and Psalm 23 may become a richer resource for life's journey. The text, in effect, moves with the community for whom it has significance.

On the other hand, community experience may change in such a way that certain texts are given a diminished status and role. Take, for example, 1 Cor 14:35: "It is shameful for a woman to speak in church; if there is anything they desire to know, let them ask their husbands at home." For those communities that ordain women, this text can never again be seen in isolation from this churchly role for women. When I read this text to my classes, it is not uncommon for snickers to roll across the room. For this community, this text is now stuck in a secondary status; a severe constraint is placed upon ways in which it can be interpreted and used. So, texts reside in communities, and meaning possibilities are deeply affected thereby.

As for community constraints on *readers,* much common ground has been achieved within both church and academy with respect to interpretive conventions and meanings of texts. In the academy, generally agreed upon, if revisable, rules for exegesis—say, form criticism—delimit the possibilities of meaning. In the church, existing conventions and confessions shape interpretation, though these can change over time, albeit slowly. For example, the way in which Baptists and Lutherans read texts on the sacraments illustrates both the range of textual meanings possible as well as the limitations within each community. So, in both academy and church, such conventions and a generally accepted range of meanings for many texts guard against arbitrariness or uncontrolled subjectivity and keep the meanings of texts reasonably stable in both kind and number.[11]

The net effect of this reality is that, when it comes to considering new meaning possibilities, a buyer's market prevails. The issue for the seller becomes one of persuasion and promotional strategies. How persuasive can I be with my interpretation of texts to potential buyers? If I want to sell my commentaries, the material will have to be presented in such a way as to appeal to buyers; if it is too eccentric or poorly argued, I won't get past a first printing. If I want to sell a church social statement with some new directions for interpretation, the biblical work will have to be persuasive, with community meanings carefully taken into account, and with a lively concern for the life, health, and flourishing of individuals and communities.

Such communities authorize or validate meanings given to texts, though among sub-communities or in times of transition within a community differing interpretations of texts vie for a place. But, if there is no group, say, the Lutheran church or the academy, which will approve an interpretation, it will not survive. At the same time, with the proliferation of subcommunities, and the increasing diversity within communities (including denominations), differing meanings of texts are on the increase; conflict within communities and the need to adjudicate among interpretations will become an increasingly complex reality for all of us. This situation is complicated by the fact that such communities cannot ever create a standard so objective as to enable a text's meaning to be accepted by every person within a community (perhaps with sectarian exceptions). We will need to learn to live with difference. It may be helpful to remember that discarded interpretations do not necessarily lose all value; they can be recycled, providing raw material for new meanings and interpretive redesign.

So, in finding a way between the two extremes of only one meaning and unlimited meanings, we have spoken of three realities: (1) The text, which is reasonably, but not entirely, stable; (2) the communities within which texts stand; and (3) the communities within which readers stand, which shape their basic sense of Scripture and faith commitments such that readings are not quite so variable as is sometimes supposed. If this complex reading situation is the reality within which we live and work, how does one talk about the authority of the text? As David Gunn states: "Reader-oriented theory legitimizes the relativity of different readings and thus threatens to unnerve conventional understandings of biblical authority."[12] If meanings of texts are various and fluid, even if not infinitely so, are all meanings of texts discerned by whoever is authoritative? If not, how does one adjudicate among meanings? Is the Bible authoritative because of the *kind* of meanings it generates, or the *number* of them? Or both?

I offer no simple response to such questions, but the next two chapters seek to work through them. At this point, eight directions for reflection might be suggested. Generally, I would claim that if we are freed up from searching for a single or original or intended meaning of the text, this will enhance the authority of the Bible in several ways.

1. It enhances the often devalued ways in which the New Testament interprets the Old Testament. The New Testament does not attend very well to the historical sense of Old Testament texts, or to a supposed original meaning. One thinks of Matt 2:15 and its quotation of Hos 11:1 regarding Jesus' flight into Egypt: "Out of Egypt I have called my son." One could say that, for the New Testament authors, it was the *text itself* that was normative, and not some inherent meaning that was to be located there. The New Testament insists upon text-centeredness, but exemplifies freedom and creativity in interpretation. The dominant historical approach has more often than not diminished the meaning possibilities of such texts. Perhaps the New Testament use of Old Testament texts provides a paradigm (albeit time-conditioned) for interpreters in every age, focusing on the text, but providing a freedom from the search for an original meaning.

2. It helps readers keep their priorities straight. According to Stanley Hauerwas, "what is at stake is not the question of the meaning of Scripture, but the usefulness of Scripture for the good ends of the Christian community,"[13] and, I would add, the world. The author-

ity of Scripture is finally a question regarding what it is good for. This would support my initial direction in thinking about the authority of the Bible, namely, its unique capacity to affect individuals and communities for good, to contribute to their life, health, and well-being.

3. It opens the texts up to a more comprehensive revelatory potential. God the Holy Spirit is not somehow confined to just one meaning in order to speak to readers. Might it be the case that the search for an original meaning finally seeks to eliminate the need for the Spirit's work through our interpretive efforts? The claim might be made: If you get that original meaning, then the Holy Spirit can speak; if you do not, then the Holy Spirit has less room to work in the hearts of those who read and hear. With an indeterminacy of meaning, the potential for what might be revealed to the reader or worked within the reader is enhanced; God is able to get through to the reader through many more avenues. Because the constituencies involved in reading the text include not just the text and the reader, but the Holy Spirit, the process is dynamic and dialogical, and generative of ever new possibilities for meaning. So, multiple meanings is an important *theological* matter, because it acknowledges the complexity of the Spirit's work in dynamic relationship with the particular situation of each and every reader.

4. Such a recognition may help relieve the anxieties associated with interpretation, the sense that, "If I do not get it right, then I have failed." It provides greater, if not unlimited, freedom to work imaginatively with the possibilities of the text. One might ask if this is not, in fact, what is happening in much preaching and teaching. Interpreters might be committed theoretically to a single or original meaning, but practically they are open to and, in fact, put forth various meanings. It would be interesting to track sermons on lectionary texts and see how textual meanings have evolved with the preachers' life experiences and those of their communities. One might even claim that this is a return to a certain form of piety, when members of a Bible study group went around the room and spoke of what the text meant to them and, not infrequently, a number of meanings emerged.

Actually, it should be of comfort that the Word of God does not consist of a single meaning from each text.

This approach does not necessarily abandon the search for truth, as if truth were only to be found in an original meaning; it recognizes that truth is a more relational category and can be received or mediated in and through various interpretations. At the same time, as we shall see in the following chapters, there is need for a center of some sort in terms of which all claims to truth are to be measured.

5. Speaking of a multiplicity of meanings helps dilute the control of academic or ecclesiastical power brokers or, for that matter, any group that would use particular interpretations to make a move to power. The emergence of new biblical interpretations among various marginalized, oppressed, or disenfranchised groups has shown how some forms of entrenched power can be subverted.

6. An increasingly diverse church facing complex challenges ought to rejoice in the indeterminacy of meaning; the church will need more readings to speak to the variety of people and situations it will face. Rather than inhibiting its basic tasks of preaching and teaching, a greater number of readings of texts will open up more possibilities for the use of the Bible in different contexts.

7. This approach demonstrates the importance of the readers' skills and competence, as well as their piety and religious imagination (and hence makes a case for theological education). The reader ought not be self-effacing, as if the only approach were simply to receive the text or to listen to the text or get out of the way of the text. Reading is a creative activity in which something of the *reader* becomes part of the meaning of the text (whether admitted or not)! If, in fact, meaning is created in the interaction between text and reader, then the full engagement of the reader is called for, and this enhances the work of the Holy Spirit in and through us.

8. An indeterminacy of meaning also has greater potential to spark the imagination. The illusion to which a single meaning may lead is that one's theology or doctrine is straight on every front; but the text so constrained can inhibit creativity and the enlivening of the imagination. A recognition of the openness of meaning in texts,

wherein various meanings constantly interact with one another, enables more new insights, gives more room for the play of the imagination, and encourages conversation.

The indeterminacy of meaning in biblical texts thus has the potential of enhancing biblical authority, providing additional avenues in and through which the Word of God can address more people, and through them enrich the life, health, and flourishing of their neighborhood, nation, and world.

CHAPTER 5

Is the Biblical Portrayal of God Always Trustworthy?

In the previous chapter I addressed some issues in culture, church, and academy that make biblical authority problematic in our time, with special attention to the indeterminacy of meaning. In the two remaining chapters I will focus on a particular issue, namely, the authority of the biblical portrayal of God, whose presence moves across the whole of Scripture. Generally speaking, how one views the authority of the Bible is closely dependent on one's imaging of God; the way a reader relates to God will decisively shape how that reader relates to the Bible.

The doctrine of God is one of the most important conversations in church and academy at the present time, and the role of the Bible in thinking through God-issues arises again and again. The biblical portrait of God has become a pressing matter, not least because numerous Bible readers, from women to pacifists to environmentalists, have raised serious questions about that portrayal. Still other readers, who seek to delineate God as a literary character,[14] are pressing traditional understandings of the God of the Bible. On the other hand, some Bible readers insist that any contemporary view of God must correspond exactly to the biblical view. For example, if the God of the Bible is presented to us in masculine terms, then for us to do otherwise is to be unfaithful, even idolatrous. Significant religious wars over the identity of the God of the Bible have just begun.

Let me put the questions this way: Does every biblical statement about God speak the truth about God? Is the Bible beyond question in what it says about God? If it is not, as we shall suggest, what criteria are used to make such a decision? And, then, what happens to biblical authority? Whether or not the Bible is always trustworthy, can post-biblical developments in our reflection about God modify or extend the biblical picture? While my concern here is to raise questions about the biblical portrayal of God, this effort is undergirded by a hermeneutics of appreciation, not just of suspicion. I raise questions because I deeply treasure these texts.

Most Christians understand that the Bible does not speak the truth about some matters. For example, for more than a century, scientific discoveries and observations have raised issues about the Bible's authority when it speaks about the natural world. In most communities an understanding has emerged that the Bible's authority does not have to do with physics or astronomy or geology or the like. Yet, even among folk who affirm this, it is amazing how a harmonization syndrome remains in place. For example, the seven days of creation in Genesis 1 are evolutionary periods. While this is a possible reading, it is more likely that the days of creation are 24-hour days. But, if the latter is the case, we have a more difficult interpretive task on our hands, given current views about the origins of the world. Given a unitary conception of truth about the world, what do we do when the Bible and science come into conflict? Must we not admit that the truth about the world may come from any number of sources, including sources outside the Bible? The Bible for all its value and reliability may not always reflect what that truth is.

Or take the issue of the historical value of biblical texts, a source of much disagreement in the churches. Many have come to recognize that the truth value of the Bible is not necessarily dependent upon the happenedness of its every report. This recognition involves two differing assessments of biblical material. On the one hand, when the Bible reports on events, its views are often not fully correspondent to what actually happened. For example, the narrator no doubt used considerable imagination in constructing a conversation between, say, David and Nathan regarding David's sin with Bathsheba; yet, the truth value of the material remains, regarding, say, the realities of sin, indictment, repentance, and forgiveness.

On the other hand, truth can be conveyed in and through types of literature that are not historical in character. Jesus' parables speak the truth even though they never happened; the book of Jonah does so as well, even though Jonah was not actually swallowed by a big fish. Yet, it is important for faith that some events of which the Bible speaks do have roots in history, for example, the Exodus or the life, death, and resurrection of Jesus.[15]

In the eyes of some, these developments regarding science or history threaten or diminish the authority of the Bible. How can it be that the Bible would be authoritative on one level but not necessarily another? That is characteristic of other books we read, of course. But some folks claim that if the truth of the Bible regarding any matter is disallowed, we move onto a slippery slope and everything in the Bible is called into question. They are right it would seem, and the biblical portrayal of God is now on the screen. The truth of the Bible regarding any topic cannot be claimed in advance or in independence from probing questions or from knowledge about the world gained from other sources. I contend that this lack of authority the Bible has with respect to certain matters helps keep our focus on its central confession regarding God and its gospel proclamation rather than on the Bible per se, important and indispensable as it is.

A myth of certainty about the Bible has often been current among us, that amid the rough seas the church and its Bible are having to endure, at least some things on the ship are tied down—like God. Even if the Bible is not fully reliable when it speaks of scientific or historical matters, can we not with certainty say that the Bible speaks the truth on all matters of faith and life? Or, more particularly, on all matters of theology, ethics, and piety? I wish it were so.

One of the first things the church ought to admit in this discussion is the long history of negative effects many biblical texts about God have had on our life together. With all the emphasis these days on what a text *does* to the reader, we should be absolutely clear: among the things the Bible has *done* is to contribute to the oppression of women, the abuse of children, the rape of the environment, and the glorification of war. It will not do to speak in any simplistic way about what the Bible *does,* and the isolated use of such language does a disservice to both Bible and church. Simply to assume that everything the Bible does is good or is good for you serves neither Bible nor church well.

It will not do to excuse the original authors because they had insufficient knowledge; the *texts* they wrote have had significant negative effects. One might claim that the problem is due to the distorted readings of sinful interpreters and not to the texts themselves, and that is often the case, but the texts cannot be freed from complicity in these matters. The texts *themselves* fail us at times, perhaps even often. The patriarchal bias *is* pervasive, God *is* represented as an abuser and a killer of children, God *is* said to command the rape of women and the wholesale destruction of cities, including children and animals. To shrink from making such statements is dishonest. To pretend that such texts are not there, or to try to rationalize our way out of them (as I have sometimes done), is to bury our heads in the sand. To continue to exalt such texts as the sacrifice of Isaac (Genesis 22), and not to recognize that, among other things, it can be read as a case of divine child abuse, is to contribute to an atmosphere that in subtle, but insidious, ways justifies the abuse of children. Both such texts and their interpreters carry deep levels of accountability for the effects they have among those who hear or read what they have to say. Lives are at stake.

We need to ask quite directly: Does not the sheer presence of such texts continue to promote abuse and violence? If the Bible has had such negative effects for over two thousand years, and still has, the issue of biblical authority becomes entwined with the issue of justice. If the Bible and its God subvert the cause of justice, what happens to authority? And permit an Old Testament student to say that the New Testament, for all of its promotion of peace, also speaks of bloody divine battles, particularly in the book of Revelation, and consigns millions of non-believers to *eternal* violence; the New Testament also has the strongest statements against the churchly leadership of women.

Massive efforts have been made in recent years to save the Bible from its patriarchy and violence. This effort has focused on certain texts that seem to break free from such perspectives, e.g., Gal 3:28, and its claim regarding the oneness of male and female in Christ Jesus. Or, in an effort to reinterpret patriarchal emphases in Genesis 2-3, appeals are made to egalitarian claims in Genesis 1 about male and female both being created in the image of God. Such texts, it is thought, can control the interpretation of the troubling texts, or at least can introduce some positive points to offset the negative ones.

Probably so. I have adopted certain of these readings in my own work; but I wonder if they are not often exegetical egg dances, seeking to rid the Bible of a patriarchy from which it cannot finally be rescued. The effort to assign such perspectives to their ancient context will not work in any simple way either, for that includes everything in the Bible. To suggest that only current experiences drive the discussion, and this too will pass, is to do violence in another way. Even to suggest that patriarchy or child abuse are passing fancies, and that someday we will once again see that the Bible was right after all, is not worthy of further conversation. The church must be up front about the Bible's complicity in such violence and seek to work from within that reality. That the presence and action of God in some texts actually reinforces this ideology is a matter to which we now turn.

Most Christians assume that whatever the Bible says about God is right or true or somehow appropriate. What God says and does in those pages is finally beyond question; no biblical text contains or conveys a contorted view of God. In speaking of such Old Testament scholars as von Rad, Zimmerli, and Westermann, David Clines claims that they "do not think the Bible ever says anything untrue about the 'real God.'"[16] More generally, it is certainly the case that their understanding of God essentially corresponds to the classical theology of the church.[17]

Such a perspective assumes, it would seem, that the sinfulness and finitude of the biblical writers is never manifest in the text with respect to theological matters. Some interpreters think that inspiration entails the screening out of sinfulness and finitude from having an effect on the theology of the text, if not on other subjects. In such a scenario, the Spirit's inspiration is selective, protecting only theological matters. Responsibility for any discontinuities between the Bible's view of God and that of its readers is to be laid at the feet of the interpreter, never the text. It is always the readers who do not get it, who seek to escape from the text's indictment, or who seek to present God in more palatable packets. Otherwise, how would it be possible for the Bible to have authority in all matters of faith and life?

Consequently, the churchly tendency is to block any challenges to biblical images for God, to screen out questions about divine accountability for moves God makes, and to come to the defense of the portrayal of God. I would claim, however, that unless one adopts a problematic view of inspiration that disallows any real participation of the human mind in writing the biblical texts, one must be open to the possibility that these sinful, finite writers did not always get their theology straight.

In reflecting about such matters, it is wise to remember that such questions and challenges regarding God are articulated within the biblical texts themselves. One thinks of questions raised in the lament psalms or the one put to God by Abraham in Gen 18:25: "Shall not the judge of all the earth do right?" regarding the fate of the righteous in the cities of Sodom and Gomorrah.[18] Abraham here asks whether God's contemplated action to destroy these cities conforms to standards of justice that God the Creator built into the world order. God honors Abraham's question by conversing with him about the fate of the cities, and God remains open to the possibility that this conversation will issue in a future for the cities different from that which God had initially contemplated.

One also thinks of the challenge Moses raises with God in the wake of the golden calf debacle in Exodus 32.[19] In their first exchange over this matter, God informs Moses that this people is about to be destroyed, and asks that Moses leave him alone. Moses, however, does not obey God's directive to leave him alone and presents a case as to why God should not destroy Israel by appealing to God's reason, reputation, and resolve. In response, God changes his mind about destroying the people. Once again, it is clear that God is responsive to human challenge; in this case, it is a challenge to God's own word. One could also discuss challenges brought by Jeremiah or Habakkuk or Job. In Elie Wiesel's words, "the Jew knows that he may oppose God as long as it is in defense of God's creation."[20]

In view of these texts, I ask: do not these divine-human exchanges provide an innerbiblical warrant for the raising and pursuing of such questions about God in every generation? Are not those modern folk who challenge the God of certain texts standing in the shoes of Abraham and Moses and Jeremiah? On the other hand, are not those who seek to *subvert* such questioning efforts being untrue to their biblical moorings? This approach suggests that the type of relationship we have with God shapes our relationship to the text. If God himself is one with whom one can dialogue and converse, this models the way in which readers ought to approach the Word of God which is the Bible.

Among the challenges one might cite in our own time are those that question the strongly patriarchal imaging of God in many texts and their history of negative effects on women. If God is imaged as a male or acts like an Israelite patriarch, and we simply accept this language, then patriarchal ways are sanctioned for the way we approach the Bible, let alone for interhuman relationships. Or, some peacemakers have questioned certain ways in which God is imaged as a warrior. At times, God functions like a typical ancient Near Eastern man of war in, say, totally destroying Israel's enemies or even Israel itself, including women, children, and animals. The question is legitimately asked: has not God thereby pointed the way for comparable human behaviors in the waging of war and for a General Patton approach in the use of the Bible?

Some interpreters respond to these and other problematic texts in a totalistic way by saying they have no continuing authority; they are of no value for the faith and life of the church, and must be set aside. Other interpreters respond in a less comprehensive way, claiming that such texts continue to be of some value. It seems to me that the totalistic approach is not helpful; it entails engagement in a Marcion-like scissors-and-paste exercise, cutting out texts here and there, ending up with a truncated canon. A more helpful way is to make distinctions within the texts themselves, even though this makes the interpretive task much more complex.

Perhaps the way in which we have often dealt with biblical views of the natural world can help point the way. We have noted that the view of the natural world in Genesis 1–2 is less than fully accurate in light of contemporary scientific understandings. At the same time, few have suggested that these verses be thrown out because of that deficiency. Rather, one moves through this lack and affirms the considerable truth about matters basic to the chapter, for example, that God is the Creator of all that is. One may even find some virtue in the contingencies. That is, the truth about the Creator is mediated in and through knowledge and language available at that time and place. This could provide a paradigm for every age; interpreters are to take the available knowledge of the world and, like their biblical predecessors, use that as a vehicle in and through which to convey other truths about the creation; for example, one could use evolution as a vehicle to speak of the complexities of God's work as Creator.

Or, we might use the example of texts from Leviticus that have to do with bloody animal sacrifices. It is clear that, for the Christian community, animal sacrifices are no longer required. At the same time, these texts remain part of our Bible; they are undergirded by a theology that, among other things, has informed and continues to inform Christian understandings of atonement and the Lord's Supper. So, once again, we make distinctions within texts with respect to the nature of the biblical authority with which we have to do.

Using this approach, how might one deal with the reading of divine child abuse in Genesis 22? God presents Abraham with a test that puts a child through a highly traumatic time, which, in view of current knowledge, we have little choice but to label as child abuse. As a consequence, the imaging of God in Genesis 22 fails us in some ways. Yet the text ought not be cut out of the canon; it still has much value for ongoing theological reflection. One thinks of the relationship between human faithfulness and divine promise, or the reality of divine testing within relationship. If we do use this text, however, we must be highly mindful of its potential negative effect on children—either directly or through abusive parents. This danger should be openly recognized, with considerable care used in preaching and teaching on the text.

This less than totalistic approach to these texts seems to me to be a more helpful way to proceed. With respect to each text, we acknowledge both its value and the dangers and/or problems it poses. But we still must ask, on what grounds do we make these *distinctions within* texts? Where can an interpreter find a neutral place on which to stand to bring such a critique? Before suggesting possible criteria, however, I address some preliminary considerations.

Some scholars claim that, by evaluating God texts, particularly those with harsher images, we domesticate God, making God more palatable to modern tastes. We are always in danger of doing this, of course, not least with images of judgment; we must move carefully, even reluctantly. We must certainly learn to read the Bible over against ourselves and not just for ourselves; we must allow the text to interrogate us, to be "in our face." But, is it not also dangerous simply to repeat texts that denigrate the place of women and portray God as an abuser and killer of children?

The image of God as Judge, indeed a judge of all of us (including every reader), must not be rendered without value; at the same time, in the tradition of Abraham and Moses, it is quite in order to raise questions about the way in which divine wrath is said to have been exercised, or about the metaphors used to depict it. For example, a number of prophetic books use female images to speak of divine judgment, where God lifts up Israel's skirts and exposes her genitalia (Isaiah 3; Ezekiel 16; 23; no such male image is used, but see Isa 8:20). God may at times be described as terrifying, but we are invited to ask whether every terroristic image the Bible uses is appropriate in our search for understanding God as fully as possible. Citing another example, it is quite in order to raise questions about the God of the story of Nathan and David in 2 Samuel 12, particularly v. 11 ("I will take your wives from before your eyes, and give them to your neighbor, and he shall lie with your wives in the sight of this very sun"). As a punishment for David's sin, fulfilled later, God gives David's women over to another man for the explicit purpose of rape. How can one affirm such a move on God's part or confess that the God in whom one believes actually does such things? We must be attentive when the Bible says something that is threatening, strange, or surprising, for that may be a word we sorely need to hear; but, at the same time, we must not fall into the trap of assuming that such texts are inevitably on track theologically.

It is important to remember that God cannot be captured in any text or language or image or system; God will always be a "problem" in one way or another. But faith does seek understanding. It is potentially just as idolatrous to claim we know so little about God as it is to claim we know so much. Either way we worship at the feet of a claim that limits God in some way. Idolatry also threatens when we interpret metaphors such as judgment or wrath in literal fashion, forgetting that such language bespeaks a no regarding God as well as a yes. But faith still seeks understanding. We want to listen for fulfillments of Jesus' promise that he would send the Spirit to lead us into all the truth (which goes beyond a personal reference to Jesus). While the Bible is indispensable in the search to understand God more fully, it is not finally sufficient, as Trinitarian formulations show. As with any interpretation, the critique of the biblical material must be brought into one's community and assessed over time as to its validity and continuing value.

We return to our question of criteria. Where can we stand in order to evaluate biblical statements about God? Generally speaking, the criteria I use throughout are creedal and ethical, both of which will be developed further in the next chapter. More particularly, the examples from Genesis 1 and 22 and Leviticus suggest that at least three factors be taken into account. These factors enable us to make some distinctions within Scripture, though this means that the issue of authority becomes more complex.

1. Nonbiblical knowledge, gained both from academic study and more general life experience. In this connection, it is important to remember that the Reformation call for *sola scriptura* (Scripture alone) was not addressed over against secular sources of information. Regarding Genesis 1–2, we make our judgments of the knowledge it conveys in part on the basis of knowledge gained from sources of truth about the world other than the Bible. Such nonbiblical sources

must be examined critically and affirmed tentatively, but their potential for enhancing our knowledge about the world has been amply demonstrated. Regarding Genesis 22, in a way parallel to the natural sciences, resources from the field of psychology have given us new insights into the effect such behavior has on children, and one could say the same for patriarchy. In addition, our own experience with abuse in its various forms has sensitized us in a way apparently not true for the narrators.

To give an innerbiblical warrant for appealing to experience in generating new reflection about God, one might cite the instance of Hagar in Genesis 16. Hagar is a woman who is ostracized from the elect family of Abraham and Sarah and banished to the wilderness. In the midst of her suffering, God comes to Hagar and gives her a word that enables a way into the future. In light of this experience, Hagar gives God a new name—El Roi. Hagar, a slave, a woman, and an outsider, uses her experience to shape new language for God.

2. Other biblical texts provide material for evaluating the portrayal of God. This can be accomplished at two levels:

A. To read the difficult texts in light of the more extensive canonical portrayal of God. Regarding Genesis 22, one thinks of texts such as Isa 49:14-15 that present a maternal God who will not desert her children ever, or the image of Jesus who takes the children into his arms and uses them as an image of the God-human relationship. More generally, the larger biblical portrait stands over against an image of God as an abuser of children. One must thus be prepared to use the principle "Scripture interprets Scripture," in such a way that Scripture interprets itself *against* itself. The internal biblical capacity to be self-critical provides a paradigm for all readers of Scripture. In this task, it must be recognized that Scripture does not interpret itself in some naked way, somehow independent of readers who have ideological commitments. Because such problematic texts continue to be used in isolation, it is important in preaching and teaching to make sure this larger canonical picture is included in one's exposition.

B. Canon within the canon. This formula asks whether a central biblical theme or textual grouping can be used to critique what other texts say. Can we use some segment of the Bible to evaluate the Bible; to cite a familiar case, can one use the gospel themes of Galatians and Romans to evaluate James and Jude? This is an essential move, and a traditional one, but not just any canon within the canon will do. It is legitimate only if one can discern an innerbiblical warrant on the basis of which to do so, not a standard from outside the Bible. This sort of move is fraught with danger, not least because any such discernment is not value-free; but such is the case with every interpretive move. All interpreters function with such a canon, though many are unaware of it or refuse to recognize it within themselves. Can a canon within the canon be discerned for evaluating texts having to do with God? This is commonly claimed to be located in the word of the gospel, that word that conveys or inculcates Christ. Scripture is in some sense subordinate to the gospel it contains and proclaims. This may be affirmed in a general way, but given the different way we treat the Old Testament these days from a traditional Christological reading, this center needs to be adjusted in more theocentric directions. This I shall seek to do in the next chapter in connection with the creedal material in Exod 34:6-7 (and its many biblical parallels).

3. Our new identity as people of God. The Bible has been shown to have a generative, life-giving quality, creating new identities for people—one of the basic reasons many consider it authoritative. Having received such an identity, such persons now stand within the same community of faith as Abraham and Moses; thereby they are drawn into a relationship with God that may include challenges and questions about God's own ways, including those found in the Bible. From within this community, persons of faith have been given an authority to speak out against whatever in the Bible may be life-demeaning, oppressive, or promoting of inequality. Such speaking will always be in need of correction, but the Bible itself gives permission, indeed an imperative, to seek to generate new, liberating structures in

the contemporary world, even if it means going beyond the truth available in the Bible on one matter or another.

Such criteria could be drawn on to assess images of God that are militaristic or patriarchal or ecologically problematic. For example, in an age where some have caught a vision of peace, many peacemakers would claim that that vision has been generated and informed by biblical texts (see Isa 2:1-4). Or some environmentalists among us have picked up on neglected biblical texts that show God's extraordinary care for the nonhuman (see Job 38–41). That many female scholars continue to value the Bible in spite of the harm it has done to women over the centuries is witness to the Bible's ability to transcend its own limitations; it does provide images of liberation, life, and equality. An example would be those Exodus 1–2 texts where women, from midwives to Pharaoh's own daughter, have a significant role to play in bringing the power structures to their knees; their actions—quite apart from any stated divine activity—subvert patriarchy and promote health and well-being.

In other words, within the Scriptures themselves a basis is given from which to bring a word against the text. This internal biblical capacity to be self-critical provides a place to stand to bring a critique against such ideological perspectives represented in the text.

These developing sensitivities ought not be credited to the Bible alone, however. Significant levels of thought and action that have contributed to peace, ecological sensitivity, and gender equality have occurred outside the bounds of church and Bible, indeed often in spite of the church and the use it has made of the Bible. I think there would be little dispute that our sensitivities in these areas have often been enhanced *first of all* by nonbiblical considerations, and then applicable biblical materials have been seen in a new light. I would claim that this is testimony to the work of God the Creator out and about in the world outside the church and its Bible, which divine work continues to be helpful to churchly theological reflections. The church has not listened to these voices as much as it should have; instead, it has amassed an amazing history of being prophetic about such issues when the crisis has passed.

Finally, one might ask: if we are to conclude that the biblical portrayal of God is not beyond question, what ought one do with these
problematic texts?

A possible parallel would be the biblical understanding of law. The
differences in the law on a subject such as slavery (compare Exodus
[21:1-11] and Deuteronomy [15:12-18]) are remarkable in that the
superseded law remains in the canon. Internal tensions and inconsis-
tencies in the law are not ironed out, nor are they considered a threat
to the law's integrity. Rather, old and new remain side by side as a
canonical witness to the process of unfolding law. In a way not unlike
the United States Constitution, the older laws that have been superseded remain as Word of God; they provide continuing points for
reflection on the development of still further laws. The old and the
new both contribute to the ongoing discussion.

In a similar way, and in conclusion, these more problematic,
indeed questionable words about God or images of God are not to
be cut out of the canon, but may serve at least six dimensions of our
conversation.

1. They remind us of the inadequacy of all of our language about
God. Every image comes up short; every metaphor has its no; every
reference to God is in some sense discontinuous with the reality that
is God. To this I return in the next chapter.

2. Such images could keep us alert to the fact that language about
God has powerful effects on people and world that are negative as
well as positive; biblical language about God can be used to promote
ideologies that do not serve life and well-being. Such texts could
remind us that language about God ought not be casual or indifferent
to developing human experience.

3. These images create theological dissonance within us; a Word of
God stands over against what we have come to know about God from
biblical and other sources. Two ways of thinking about this dissonance
seem possible:

A. Kathryn Darr puts it this way: "Sometimes, we continue to
embrace hurtful texts not because we affirm their answers,
but rather because they force us to confront the important

questions."[21] This perspective, of course, assumes that we will recognize the hurtful texts for what they are. We have not always so recognized them.

B. Such texts put the fear of God in the reader and drive him or her to a newer Word of God, especially that new word embodied in the Christ. But this approach assumes that such texts speak an appropriate word about God; biblical words about God that are deeply disjunctive from the basic biblical witness to God ought not put the fear of God in anyone.

4. Such an approach could enhance the dialogical relationship with the text more generally. That is, the engagement with such questionable texts provides a model for our ongoing interactive approach to all biblical texts. This would mean that a proper approach to the text is not one of passivity or submission or simply "listening"; it is one of full engagement, recognizing that meaning does not reside in the text, but emerges in the interaction of text and reader.

5. These problematic images of God keep us mindful of the fact that every presentation of the Word of God will bring forth the contingent and the constant. Both are necessary if the Word about God is to reach into ever new times and places. Those who are bearers of the Word of God need not be reminded that the language, concepts, and images used may in time be viewed as deeply problematic. That is the price paid for seeking to bring the constant into language for our own time.

6. The friction created by the rub between such questionable texts and the language of God we do use is capable of sparking our imaginations, getting us to think of God in new ways. Indeed, it may invite us to rethink and even revise our *present* language about God. We are thereby called upon to ask into the appropriateness of every formulation about God we speak or confess and its adequacy to Bible, tradition, and experience. These texts may enable us to be more attuned to the Spirit's leading us into new ways of thinking about the God in whom we believe and whom we confess to be the light and life of the world.

CHAPTER 6

The Authority of the Bible
and Imag(in)ing God

In chapter 5 I asked whether the biblical portrayal of God is always trustworthy. This lecture extends this concern about the God of the Bible, but it focuses on the question as to whether this portrayal is coherent and, if not, in what sense it can be considered authoritative.

The God of much churchly tradition is remarkably similar to the generic god of the average person on the street. God is given the traditional attributes of omnipotence, omniscience, immutability, impassibility, atemporality, etc. Yet the Bible often gives testimony to a God who does not fit those categories; it speaks about God in ways that the church has often ignored or set aside. Take the God of the flood story: God expresses sorrow and regret; God decides to blot out every living thing and then doesn't do so when Noah finds favor with God; God promises never to do this again, thereby placing eternal limitations on the divine response to human wickedness. To this might be added: God is affected by people's prayers (Exod 32:11-14), or God tests people because the divine knowledge of future human behaviors is less than absolute (Gen 22:12). Indeed, I think the God of *most* biblical texts is not impassible or immutable or atemporal or omnipotent or omniscient, at least in any conventional understanding of those terms.

But, if *some* biblical texts support traditional understandings, how does one work with these differences in any move to a biblical theology or a contemporary formulation? If there are not only multiple meanings of texts, but multiple theologies, do we let people just pick and choose the theology they like, and name it all biblical? But, if we have a biblical theological pluralism, then the question of authority gets more complicated: are *all* such biblical theologies authoritative?

Or are distinctions to be made among theologies? If so, does the Bible itself prioritize them? Are differing biblical theologies pertinent for different times and places? Or is the authority of the Bible finally dependent upon its containing a univocal understanding of God?

Timothy Beal states this issue from one perspective: "Almost invariably, modern biblical criticism—especially modern biblical theology—has been driven by a desire for *univocality*; that is, a desire to identify a single, stable, divine character who remains fundamentally the same in every piece of biblical discourse."[22] He claims that this desire is misplaced and seeks to show that the portrayal of the biblical God across the canon is profoundly ambivalent. But he leaves us there.

This perspective is implicit in many recent readings of biblical narratives by literary critics. These critics often set aside traditional readings of God quite deliberately and seek to forge new ones. God is analyzed and assessed as any other character might be, and some of the results are rather startling to traditional readers. Generally, I would say this is a salutary development; many insights will no doubt emerge from this approach. At the same time, significant issues have emerged regarding the way in which God is depicted as a character in the story.[23] I give two examples of recent readings of God as a character.

First, I look at the depiction of the God in Genesis 2–3, assisted by the readings of David Gunn, Danna Fewell, and James Barr.[24] A modern reader might understand the way God responds to Adam and Eve if the sin were like Cain's murder of Abel or the violence before the flood. But eating a piece of fruit? It sounds like a divine sting operation. Parents know that one way to get a child interested in something is to prohibit it. To quote Barr: "God has made an ethically arbitrary prohibition and backed it up with a threat to kill which, in the event, he does nothing to carry out." In all this, it sounds like God wants to keep human beings servile, not only taking care of his private garden, but keeping them ignorant. Moreover, God does not give counsel to Eve in the midst of the temptation as God later would help her son Cain; God lets Adam and Eve fend for themselves in the midst of a moment that would have devastating consequences. God seems content to go wandering in the garden in the cool of the day. Upon becoming suspicious, God asks simplistic questions to find out what has been going on. Having discovered them, God passes out "humiliations, limitations, and frustrations" as if they were a dime a dozen. God thereby makes animals and humans hate each other, makes women bear children in pain, gives the man dominion over her, and makes the man's work full of hardship. Then, as if to make up for the divine outburst, God takes pity on the humans and makes some clothes for them, only to turn around and kick them out of the garden. This God is so self-protective. God wants to keep the knowledge of good and evil to himself, and having failed to do that, God expels the humans from the garden lest they become immortal like God is. And then God rolls out all the heavenly armor to make sure they do not try to sneak back in.

Second, listen to Philip Davies on the Abraham story in Genesis 12–25. For Davies, this is "a story of male bonding, the story of a relationship between two males, Abraham and his God Yahweh . . . , who, from beginning to end, try to bluff each other. Neither is entirely successful; each is too clever to be taken in by the other, but they both keep trying anyway, because that is the way males behave. . . . The story of Abraham is a delightful anatomy of a certain kind of male twosome, two macho characters who come together for their own purposes and go along with each other because of mutual interest, a liking for each other's bluffing and a certain sneaky regard for each other's deviousness." [25]

Davies goes on to speak of a moral of the Abraham story: "Don't trust this God. He doesn't trust you and won't tell you the truth. He is in the business of making promises that are never fulfilled. Abraham . . . recognized that the promises were a kind of running gag, no more. Deities, like politicians, try to keep us dangling in the hope of things to come. . . . Be wise, like Abraham. Take everything this (or any) deity says with a pillar of salt. . . . If you really believe in what he says, you will lose. But if you call his bluff, pretend to go along with him while keeping your own counsel and taking whatever he decides to give you, you will prosper. If he wants to bless you, do not object, but let it not deter you from your own course or seduce you into groveling gratitude."

Are these plausible readings? They should certainly be allowed to compete in the marketplace to see if they catch on and to see what good they bring. There they will encounter other readings, and if in the mix they do take hold in some community, that would authorize them as valid for that community. Yet, because interpretations are not as authoritative as the texts themselves, that community, if it is to have integrity, must be alert to other readings of these texts and be ready to revise its own reading or reject it altogether.

In such an assessment, what questions are important to ask of each reading? They include: Does it attend well to the details and dynamics of the text itself? Is it coherent and intelligible? Is it true to human experience? Does it function primarily to promote a certain ideology or to keep a certain group in power? What is it good for? What value does it have for people's lives? Is it ethically responsible? Does it contribute to life, health, and the flourishing of human and non-human communities? How well does it correspond to other witnesses about God, especially the God whom we know from biblical confessional statements and the God whom we know in Jesus Christ? We will keep these questions in mind as we make our way through the following considerations.

First, narrative criticism gives us several questions to address the text in assessing the value of its God-talk:

1. Point of view. When God is characterized in the text, whose point of view is being expressed?[26] Basically, three: (a) The narrator speaks of God. These references seem especially valuable, because they express the narrator's own point of view. (b) God says certain things about himself. While these words probably represent the narrator's view, that the words are placed in God's mouth gives them a special status. (c) A character says certain things about God. These references are often difficult to assess. The theology voiced by one character does not necessarily have the same value as that voiced by another. The narrator may agree or disagree with the theology voiced by a character. One thinks of the theology of Job's friends, or the serpent in the garden, or Jacob's uncle Laban, or even that of Jacob at times (see Gen 30:2)! In such cases, biblical texts may not tell the truth about God.

2. Rhetoric. Besides point of view, another complexifying factor in assessing the character of God is the nature of the rhetoric used. One cannot always be certain how words by God or about God are to be interpreted, whether literally or ironically or hyperbolically. Such an assessment has to be made *before* one seeks to determine their theological value. What about the theology of, say, the lament psalms? Inasmuch as they are spoken in situations of deep distress, is their understanding of God comparable to what moderns might say in a tight spot, but would never say in a carefully formulated statement?

In this regard, it is instructive to observe how interpreters handle difficult texts. To cite one example, in Brueggemann's interpretation of Exodus 11–12,[27] the God who mediates the killing of Egyptian children is shown to be a God who cannot be domesticated. Probably so. Yet he insists that this material is liturgical pageant. His genre designation means that he does not take the text as straightforward description, and this introduces more qualification in his characterization of God than he seems willing to admit.

3. Biblical characters, God included, are literary constructs; they are not "flesh-and-blood" personalities. Words on the page are not the same as characters in real life. The characters portrayed in the pages of the Bible are not the actual Moses or the actual Jesus or the actual God. The God portrayed in the text does not fully correspond to the God who transcends the text, who is a living, dynamic reality that cannot be captured in words on a page. God can give himself to us in, with, and under the text, but that God does not fully correspond to the character portrayed.

Among the reasons for this slippage are gaps and silences in the presentation of characters; these encourage readers to imagine, to speculate, even to psychologize about what makes them tick. Through the centuries, readers have been quick to fill in the gaps and to give voice to characters, including God. We have used our imaginations to read between the lines, to wonder about ambiguities and uncertainties, and to decide among possibilities in the portrayal of God.[28]

It is difficult to discern the relationship between the textual God and the actual God, the God who is a character in the text and the

God who transcends it. How is one to proceed? There are two ditches to avoid:

1. To identify the real God with the God who is textually embodied. This position would claim that the text somehow captures or encloses God, tells it like it really is with God. But such an approach would in effect deny that the God in whom people believe transcends the text. The Bible does not give us an unmediated vision into the throne room of God, a window overlooking heavenly landscapes. The knowledge of God, indeed God's own self, *is* mediated to us through the text, yet in some basic sense, the God in whom we believe is *not* the God portrayed in the Bible. According to Fewell and Gunn, "The notion that the figure God in the biblical text is actually God who is worshiped by Jewish and Christian believers seems to us to be, ironically, a form of idolatry such as biblical voices constantly warn against."[29] Perspectives such as this give many recent interpreters their freedom in interpreting God as a character.

Another possible effect of identifying the textual God and the actual God would be to disallow readers' questions about their relationship. Because the textual God and the actual God are not identical, the *text pushes beyond itself and implicitly invites questions about God* (in ways similar to metaphor, as we shall see). In what ways is the actual God different from the textual God? In view of the slippage between them, all imaging of the God of the Bible has been and will be imaginative to some degree. The text itself thus implicitly invites us to *imagine God,* to imagine more adequate language and images for God, to imagine language that is more attuned to new times and places. This act of imagining will take into account ongoing experience with God and world under the guidance of the Holy Spirit. The text mediates that encounter, but the ongoing experience may enable one to imagine God in ways truer to the actual God than the textual God allows, and one thinks of Trinitarian formulations.

2. The second ditch to avoid: to deny *any* relationship between the literary character and the real God. One form of this position is to deny that the text refers to any reality beyond itself; the text is a closed and self-sufficient world. As we have noted, however, the very nature

of the text is an invitation beyond itself; the text itself insists that it is not a self-enclosed world. The reality of God cannot, of course, be demonstrated from the text. No matter how authoritative the Bible is believed to be, to speak of the reality of God is to move *beyond the Bible* and to make a fuller confession of faith than the Bible contains.

Another form of this denial would be to claim that God is so radically transcendent that no text can, in the final analysis, say anything about God. I claim, however, that, while God transcends the text, the text does convey knowledge of the actual God. In seeking to portray this God, however, we must be aware of the imaginative character of the enterprise, check our efforts with what other readers have discerned, and remember that the tradition and community in which we stand will shape our construal of God in ways beyond our knowing.

Are there no constraints on the imagination in all this? As we have noted, text, community, and innerbiblical warrants provide some direction. Generally, it might be said that the God who is imagined should be portrayed in terms of the basic thrust of the character portrayed in the text. Yet, this is complicated by our recognition that some biblical characterizations of God fail us, and so a contemporary imag(in)ing of God may well stand over against a given text. A most important resource in this imaginative effort will be the generalizations about God to which the Bible bears witness, to which we shortly turn.

But, first, some words about metaphor.[30] All metaphors or images for God bespeak both a yes and a no. That is, at the basic thrust of the analogy metaphors correspond to the reality that is God (the yes of the metaphor), but they also bespeak a no, for God outdistances all our images. For example, the use of the metaphor "father" for God, with all of its continuities with the reality that is God, also bespeaks a no; for example, God does not beget children.

As with the textually embodied God of the narrative, the task of discerning the yes and the no in the metaphor is difficult. Not all metaphors have the same value; they have varying degrees of revelatory capacity. For example, Hosea's image of God as parent (11:1) has more value than does his image of God as dry rot (5:12). Some metaphors bespeak so much no that they obscure who God is (e.g., God is a killer of children); others are used so often that they may throw the image of God out of balance (e.g., father); others may need revision in view of a new context. For example, the negative images of divine judgment in terms of female sexuality, cited above, are such that it may be very important to say no to their use altogether. These images, after all, are not "mere metaphors" but have great impact on our thinking and feeling and being; they sink deep into our selves and shape us in ways beyond our knowing. But all metaphors, whether of high value or low, are only partial visions into the truth about God; *no metaphor is fully correspondent to the actual God.*

To return to our discussion of narrative, sometimes it is suggested that the narrative discloses a story world into which its readers are invited.[31] This story of the interaction between God and God's people is said to reveal the basic identity and character of God. But, it would seem, this perspective is too dependent upon a certain construal of the story. If the story is read differently and God is characterized in nontraditional terms—in ways we have noted—then on what grounds is one reading of the story chosen over another? In such a scenario, one ends up pitting readings of the story against one another, and in such an encounter, the traditional reading will win out, at least for the community that holds it dear. To use other language, some people lodge the authority of the Bible in the Bible's capacity to draw its readers into a certain narrative world. But, if that construal of the narrative is called into question and a different portrayal of God emerges, such as those we have noted above, then how does one assess which characterization of God is authoritative beyond a simple appeal to one's own reading of the story?

The way we have worked with narratives (in terms of textual God and actual God) is not unlike the way in which one works with metaphors, with biblical images for God. Yet the metaphors bring the reader one step further along in providing the groundwork for the task of imagining God. Indeed, certain ruling metaphors or generalizations provide a key place from which to assess the adequacy of the readings noted above. The generalizations made about God may grow out of the story, but they take an additional step. By being drawn into creedal statements, a literary genre that indicates that explicit truth-claims about God are being made, they provide more yes with respect to the reality of God.

How does one determine the identity of these ruling metaphors? While objective criteria are not available in making such a determination, the following categories seem most fundamental: (1) pervasiveness; (2) literary genre; and (3) tradition.[32] Among these, genre seems most important; those images of God that are drawn into the creedal and hymnic genres are thereby deemed to have an especially high value by the community of faith; they make key truth-claims about God. The most common creedal or confessional statement in the Old Testament is found in Exod 34:6-7,[33] and it echoes throughout the Psalter in particular:

> The Lord, the Lord,
> a God merciful and gracious,
> slow to anger,
> and abounding in steadfast love and faithfulness,
> keeping steadfast love for the thousandth generation,
> forgiving iniquity and transgression and sin,
> yet by no means clearing the guilty.

These are deep underlying assumptions about God; they pervade the canon and its various traditions; they inform and bring considerable coherence to biblical God-talk. From a canonical perspective, every biblical image of God finally must be qualified by these generalizations. God is not simply father; God is a certain kind of father. God is a loving father, always. Only such generalizations, irreducible to story form, enable one to discern continuities in the story, to spot something strange or new, or to realize when an objective has been reached. They give internal directions for interpreting the God of the narrative. The God of the narrative could be characterized in various ways, but these metaphors make truth claims that give specific direction to one's interpretation. These truth-claims regarding the *kind of God* active in Israel's life provide a hermeneutical key to the story, delimiting possibilities of meaning. A simple narrative world will not do.

Through much of this century, confessional recitals of God's mighty acts in Israel's history (e.g., Deut 26:5-9; Josh 24:2-13) have been thought to provide the clue to Israel's God-talk. These recitals are important in assessing the God of the narratives, but they are insufficient, for they do not often make clear what kind of God is acting, e.g., a God who saves could be capricious and unloving and unjust. Moreover, the recitals do not provide continuity across the entire Old Testament. Several texts, especially in literature that spans the exile, indicate that Israel is to forget the saving events of the past and look to the future for such divine action (Jer 23:7; cf. 3:16, 16:14-15; Isa 43:18-19). That which provides for the continuity between past and future is not Israel's story. Rather, it is certain basic convictions regarding God. These convictions can be seen clearly in the most oft-repeated Old Testament confession regarding God, quoted above, Exod 34:6-7 (and its parallels).

This kind of statement has been neglected in Old Testament scholarship, perhaps because of its more abstract, even propositional character. Its confessional form, moreover, making sharp and succinct truth-claims about God, has probably also contributed to its neglect. But these materials are important for balancing the focus on story in the historical recitals. It is just such truth-claims about God that enable Israel to see the continuity in its own story and to be carried across those times when the story seems to have broken off. The God confessed by Israel remains constant across the story's interruptions, especially the chasm of exile. The book of Lamentations, which never appeals to God's actions in Israel's past, makes this kind of confession (3:20-32). In the midst of the great gulf between past and future, the hope of Israel is not to be placed in its own story, but in the kind of God whom it confesses. Hence, the God who is the subject of sentences in the narrative is to be understood fundamentally in terms of those generalizations.

Insight into the character of God comes to Israel through the years along an amazing array of avenues. The key salvific events may be the primary reality for generating metaphors, but they are not alone. Indeed, the confession in Exodus 34 follows upon Israel's sin with the golden calf. If all that Israel could have said was that God acted in redemptive ways, then hope could have been an occasional thing. Who knows what God will act like the next time around? The crucial confession has to do with the *kind* of God God has been, is, and will be. God is faithful, loving, gracious, and righteous; hence, there is hope. So, the generalizations are crucial for evaluating any reading of the narrative. Finally, they make an intelligible and reasonably coherent narrative world possible.

The combination of these generalizations and the historical recitals, integrated in some texts, suggests that together they represent some measure of unanimity regarding the characterization of God amid the Bible's theological pluralism; in effect, they constitute a metaphorical canon within the canon. Just as the historical recitals confess those events in Israel's history that were constitutive of its identity, so also the generalizations about God provide the confessional clue for determining the basic character of the God of the story. Together they delineate the parameters within which a legitimate biblical theological pluralism can operate.

So, in the midst of all that makes for process and pluralism, there is that which is utterly constant in Israel's claims about the God in whom it believes. That which provides for the most fundamental continuity through the centuries is not the story of ever-lapsing Israel nor the heritage of faith that is always being reformulated; it is the history of a certain kind of God who will always, come what may, execute justice and love the stranger (Deut 10:18). God's salvific will is never diminished; God's righteousness is never compromised; God's faithfulness will never waver; God's steadfast love endures forever. God will be this kind of God wherever God is being God. But there are also those images of God that move around with people and their stories, and are affected by them (e.g., the wrath of God is always provoked).[34]

I return to a brief evaluation of the Genesis readings we noted at the beginning of this chapter. It is ironic that such readings seem grounded in a surface reading of the text. A literalistic hermeneutic seems to have returned, but with the powers of deconstruction at its disposal. More problematic is the refusal to grant any content to the character of God based on material outside this story, even from Genesis 1, let alone giving God any privileged position. The narratives are treated in isolation, as self-contained entities, with no attention given to the text as a whole and hence to generalizations about God sprinkled throughout the larger narrative. In effect, these readers are creating a greater and greater distance between the textual God and the actual God. In doing this, so much distance could be created between the two that the links are increasingly difficult to discern; the no of the narrative is shouted so loudly that the yes can hardly be heard.

One cannot help but wonder whether some readers seek to cope with the God of the text (and the God who *is*) by reductionistically confining God within isolated narratives. Is it a matter of making God more manageable, of getting out from under what is perceived to be a troubling presence? Perhaps this is so, but the more likely motivation is an attempt to break down the negative effects of centuries of using the text to promote patriarchal and other wrong-headed interpretations of God. But now, in this important enterprise, how such readers speak of God is a matter of no little responsibility. One should be alert to possible new kinds of readings that could have effects just as life-negating in the long run as certain traditional ones have been.

From another angle, many narrative critics depend upon the traditional view of God for their character analysis. That is, they seek to show, directly or indirectly, that the God of many Old Testament texts does not correspond very well to the God of classical theism. Nowadays, however, this is a comparatively easy task, with increasing numbers of theologians putting forth formulations that are truer to the biblical moorings. The God of the Old Testament often contributes positively to this discussion: Yahweh is a passionate God who enters into lively conversations with people like Abraham and Moses, who gets jealous, who repents of something said or done, who is genuinely influenced by people's prayers.[35] What would these narrative readers do if they more often recognized this theological sea change? These critics sometimes charge that those who object to their characterizations of God are engaged in "a defense of God." But this critique usually assumes that classical theism is the elephant in the room.

Those who interpret the Bible have a responsibility, not simply to themselves, but to those who read and hear what they have to say. No reading is value-free; how we interpret will in one way or another promote the personal and social values we hold dear. All readings have political force. Hence a key question to be asked of every inter-pretation: What will its effects be? What is at stake if I interpret the text in a certain way? What are my responsibilities as an interpreter? What ideology might I be promoting? Will my interpretation con-tribute to the life and well-being of others, and to the flourishing of community, or will it serve only to keep the powerful in their places or establish new centers of power? As biblical scholars and churchly leaders our readings will function as a role model for others; this makes for a certain urgency with respect to our sense of responsibil-ity in biblical interpretation.[36]

If these readings of the text, and these various characterizations of the God of the text, stand in some conflict with one another, what do we do in thinking through issues of authority and contemporary the-ological formulation?

It seems to me that we have three basic options:

1. Let theologians pick and choose among texts about God according to their own likes and dislikes, in terms of whatever tradi-tion within which they may be working or community to which they belong. The value of this option would be that differing formulations regarding God may be required for differing contexts, to meet differ-ing needs of people in various times and places. This would place a high premium on the skill of discernment with respect to contextual needs and an openness to make adjustments in theological formula-tion in view of those needs. The disadvantage is that the result would be (and I think in fact often is) a biblical-theological cacophony, with no little confusion as to just who the God of the Bible really is.

2. Insist that these biblical differences be adjudicated somehow so as to emerge with a univocal picture of God in any biblical theology or systematic formulation (e.g., have ruling metaphors qualify all other metaphors decisively). The value of this option is that the church would present a coherent and unified theological front on

such a fundamental issue as the identification of the God whom it trusts and worships. One might claim that this also has significant implications for mission, though the missional point of the first option may be more compelling.

One disadvantage of this option would be the temptation to harmonize the text's portrait of God, and such an effort would often lean in the direction of traditional formulations. Fewell and Gunn put it well: "God will exhibit traits such as being always completely good, just, and in the right, as well as all-powerful, totally in control of all that happens, and knowing all (past, present and future)." And so, "thoughts, feelings, and actions that appear to conflict with such expectations (jealousy, anger, violence, favoritism, change of mind, lack of knowledge, failure to anticipate developments) are then either ignored or rationalized as good, just, etc., or these values are redefined to fit the behavior of the divinity."[37]

3. A third option seems preferable. Seek a unified portrayal of God, but with the understanding that some biblical texts will just not fit; they provide some ongoing over-againstness to that portrayal. The continuing value of these texts is that they constantly challenge the reader to reexamine any construal. Another value is the recognition that the biblical differences have the capacity to spark the theological imagination. It is in the clash of the differences, in combination with the continuing work of the Spirit, that new and more profound knowledge of God can become available. Hence, I seek to present a unified portrayal of God to the modern world, but I recognize that the texts cannot so neatly be lined up behind such a portrayal as I might like and that the ongoing struggle with the differences leads one onward in the search for the truth about God.

Authority is related to these various biblical theologies in different ways, but all will have some authoritative role to play. Those perspectives that are not caught up in the prevailing theology may function as a gadfly or an ongoing challenge to rethink existing formulations. Or, they may be given a kind of back-burner status, perhaps to function at another time and place. So, finally, the God in whom I believe is not somehow confined to the images available in these texts or to the story presented there. The God who comes in, with, and under the text is greater than the portrayal of any biblical text or narrative, indeed, greater than any God-composite one might discern from the Bible as a whole. As a result, while the Bible functions as an indispensable resource for generating ever new reflections about God, the yield from such reflections has extended and will extend beyond biblically envisioned possibilities—witness Trinitarianism.

We have noted that the Bible's authority is derivative, that it derives its authority from the God to whom it witnesses. Now, if God is perceived to be distant, aloof, and removed from life—especially in times of suffering and grief—then the authority of the Bible may become authoritarian; and, in this day and age, its authority would often be diminished. On the other hand, if God is the kind of God who is genuinely engaged in relationship with people and world, then our relationship to the Bible would commonly have the character of a conversation or dialogue, "an asking and a listening that is open to the faith claims of the text, and with contemporary experience in view."[38] In other words, the kind of God in whom we believe will shape how we relate to the Bible, as well as how we view the nature of biblical authority. What the church must be about is articulating an understanding of God that is not only able to strike home in the hearts of people but is able to catch them up in the divine-human dialogue, mediated by the biblical texts. The church cannot demonstrate the authority of the Bible; it can only issue a call to enter into a community where the Word of God is preached and taught and we are invited into an ongoing conversation with the biblical witness. Then, and only then, will the Bible be seen as having an authority worthy of our attention.

By Karlfried Froehlich

READERS OF THE TWO ESSAYS IN THIS VOLUME WILL FIND THAT BOTH authors address the same topic and discuss the same questions, which the Committee had formulated for them to consider. It will also be clear, however, that they do so with very different concerns on their minds and different frames of reference. This may be due to their respective disciplines. Professor Fretheim is an Old Testament scholar of note, and my area of competence is church history. I admire my biblical colleague who fearlessly tackles pressing theological issues in church and academy head-on. Historians are not accustomed to doing that. They introduce caveats, they digress, and they always introduce more factors to be considered. Still, the reader must feel somewhat bewildered, like being a passenger on two ships each of which pursues its own course in the darkness of the night. Here and there the night is temporarily illumined by sudden bursts of light that reveal that the two ships at least are sailing close to each other in the same waters. I certainly resonate with Fretheim's preliminary definition of biblical authority: it is "the Bible's unique capacity to mediate God's judgment and grace, which can effect life and salvation for individuals and communities" (p. 82). I also agree that the question of biblical authority is "most basically an inside, churchly conversation," predicated on the personal confession that the God of the Bible is my own God. Obviously, we share some very important presuppositions. Even more surprising to me is the discovery that our conclusions match as well. His final point that "the church cannot demonstrate the authority of the Bible; it can only issue a call to enter into a community where the Word of God is preached and taught and we are invited into an ongoing conversation" (p. 126) parallels almost verbatim the conclusion of my own argument in the final lecture (p. 60). The two ships seem to be bound for the same port, after all.

Why then the striking discrepancies in mood and content? It seems that the differences reflect those different concerns and frameworks I just mentioned. My colleague is much concerned about a simple fact: Rather than solving any problems, the Bible has come to be a problem itself. It no longer enjoys any special privilege in determining the rules of life in our society. Bible knowledge has decreased, and the good book is mainly used for the partisan purposes of the power brokers. Among academics, the Bible is simply one source among others for the study of religion. Far from deploring these trends, Fretheim boldly accepts them and relentlessly pursues their logic to disturbing consequences.

He sees the problem mainly as a problem of biblical *interpretation:* with the loss of confidence in the one intended sense of biblical texts as established by historical-critical exegesis, any hope for a normative interpretation is nipped in the bud. The reader must expect and live with a multiplicity of possible interpretations of each and every part of the Bible. But the problem reaches deeper. With the necessity of a hermeneutic of suspicion, it has become clear that the Bible's talk about God is not only ambiguous and contradictory but often plainly wrong on ethical, logical, and experiential grounds. Fretheim wants to protect the "real" God from an unworthy image, from the caricature of the "textual" God projected by a highly suspect Bible. Thus, his reflections on biblical authority are part of a more comprehensive theological agenda the technical term for which is "theodicy," the defense of God in the face of human doubt and anger at an all-too-human Bible. The deep concerns of an engaged teacher of the Bible are expressed powerfully and passionately in what the author says.

From my point of view, Fretheim's concerns illustrate once more the problem of the middle term, which is faulted almost by definition if something goes wrong in the tension between two poles. He has forcefully exposed what he and others regard as being wrong with the Bible. He also sees clearly how this problem problematizes the one pole, God. The other pole seems to be overlooked, however. Is there *no* problem with the autonomous postmodern Bible reader whom my colleague wants to please? For Fretheim, the reader has mainly inalienable rights and legitimate warrants for complaints. I am unhappy with the resolute endorsement of this "autonomous self" as the true partner in the relationship between God and the human reader mediated through the Bible. If my assumption is correct that the rescue of the real God from the tyranny of the biblical text is at the heart of Fretheim's argument, then the frame of reference for his enterprise is unabashed Christian apologetics.

It was Karl Barth who made me aware of the dangers of an apologetic stance informing the church's theology. The contemporary world with its assumptions, values, and norms is allowed to dictate the rules of the game. Apologists listen for clues from outside the church, where their presumed dialogue partners are located, as if they themselves were located out there also. Many of the details that irk me in reading Fretheim's lectures may find their explanation in this framework: the easy identification of sexist language with the phenomenon of patriarchy, as if a linguistic purge could effect the change of heart required to overcome that system's social consequences; the simplistic application of the notion of "child abuse" to a story like Genesis 22, as if the recent popular awareness of this evil must take precedence over the far deeper issues of human experience that this story has raised throughout history; the utilitarian restriction of criteria for "assessing" the truth of the Bible to its usefulness—"what is it good for?" (p. 114), as if modern notions of "life, health, and the flourishing of human and nonhuman communities" were self-evident and therefore absolute values.

As a consequence of the apologetic framework, Fretheim is far too optimistic, it seems to me, about a genuine Christianity without the authority of the Bible (or with a much diminished one), and far too pessimistic about the prospect of a Christian church with it. If one attempts to speak in the church as if one's vantage point were *outside,* one is bound to raise false hopes. Getting rid of "power brokers" or of a "prevailing ideology" in biblical interpretation does not mean that there will be no power brokers and no ideological agendas. Exposing and purging violence from the Bible does not make violence less prevalent in our secularized society. The charge of "complicity" hurled at the Bible seems rather naive if one considers the actual causes of social evil in our time. And the courting of the autonomous individual who has the right and authority to speak out "against whatever in the Bible may be life-demeaning, oppressive, or promoting of inequality" (p. 108) sounds hypocritical when such individuals are left to their own standards of judging the evidence. In its striving for solidarity with the contemporary world, this kind of apologetics is forced to appeal to the pride of a postenlightenment mentality as the trusted guide to find a solution to all the problems it perceives. It must hail as progress every move "beyond"—beyond the Bible into a realm of supposedly more reliable truth; beyond the exegetical tradition into the potential of unbridled imagination; beyond the strictures of biblical language into the righteous purity of nonoffensive wording; beyond the unpalatable "textual God" to the "actual God" of the dearest dreams of contemporary idealism. It is my fear that, in endorsing a framework such as this, we become the victims of an ephemeral self-delusion. And the more honest the attempt to identify with the contemporary world, the more hollow the ring of any affirmation about "community," about a church, which, as Fretheim himself suggests, should function as a regulating, norm-setting power over against any reliance on the unquestioned values of modernity.

On the other end of the spectrum, the apologetic framework has led my colleague into far too pessimistic an assessment of the potential of living with an authoritative Bible in the church today. With all the problems of a very human book, even the most casual observer cannot fail to see that the Bible has been a source of constant renewal and reform of institutions and individual lives through many centuries. With all the problems of competing interpretations, the presence of those old biblical writings, however unstable one judges text and readers to be, has been, and still is unleashing an immense creativity in understanding the message in order to make the gospel a living and life-affirming voice. With all the problems of an irredeemably sexist language that keeps alive the memory of the barbarian past from which our present linguistic culture arose, the Bible, its tales, its metaphors, and it images give words to the innermost experience of countless men and women, the experience of self and of God. With all the problems of the "textual God," the "actual God" who is confessed in the Bible always had a way of cutting through the limitations of the human language through which he chose to communicate with humans so that the word of judgment and grace could be heard. Fretheim knows all this; he even affirms it. But the apologetic framework inevitably gets in the way. Apologetic zeal gives in too quickly to the instincts of contemporary mentalities without allowing room for their critique by the biblical witness. The author concludes that the responsible discernment of the center of the Scriptures points to the "real God" as the God of love, of affirmation, of mercy and grace. This God, of course, has been part of the church's proclamation all along, but the description also caters directly to the religious instincts of our generation. Bonhoeffer called it "cheap grace." Fretheim wants to assure this generation that they have nothing to fear, that this image of God indeed is the "constant." The biblical talk about God's wrath and indignation, according to him, is not of the same order; it is "contingent," and therefore dispensable, not part of the essence.

I wonder what Martin Luther would say to this assessment. With Luther, I would have to conclude that it is not only unscriptural but also goes against human experience, Luther's as well as mine, and faith experience is, after all, where the search for the truth about God in the Bible starts: "The kind of God in whom we believe will shape how we relate to the Bible" (p. 126). Personally, I am glad that, by being forced back, time and again, to the offensive, immoral, ambiguous, always contingent God-language of the Bible, I am returning to the point from which a fresh start will be possible. Here, the shortcomings of my own vision can be corrected, and my experience can find ever deeper expression in language and images that have the capacity to grow on me.

The acute embarrassment over the Bible may, of course, become so intolerable that one simply wants to leave the Bible behind and emigrate. One can emigrate into women-church, religion departments, new age communities, and a host of other social configurations that promise more direct access to the Spirit obscured in the book. In a church that is confessionally committed to the Bible as its norm and rule, we are stuck with it. We may consider this situation with gnashing teeth and clenched fist as our being condemned to live with a hopelessly flawed source of authority for ever. Alternately, we can regard the need to struggle with this uncomfortable Bible as a privilege, a chance for ever new discoveries and ever new beginnings in the dialogue the living, eternal God has initiated for our benefit. It is we, not God, who need a middle term in order to hear the Word of God. I assume, and there is much evidence for the assumption, that my colleague joins me in preferring the latter perspective.

1. Maurice Wiles, "Scriptural Authority and Theological Construction: The Limitations of Narrative Interpretation," in *Scriptural Authority and Narrative Interpretation,* ed. Garrett Green (Philadelphia: Fortress Press, 1987), 43-44. I am indebted for my analysis in this segment to Darrell Jodock, *The Church's Bible: Its Contemporary Authority* (Minneapolis: Fortress Press, 1989).

2. David J. A. Clines, *What Does Eve Do to Help? And Other Readerly Questions to the Old Testament* (JSOTSupp 94; Sheffield: *Journal for the Study of the Old Testament,* 1990), 123.

3. Walter Brueggemann, "James L. Crenshaw: Faith Lingering at the Edges," *Religious Studies Review* 20 (1994), 103; cf. also his *Texts under Negotiation* (Minneapolis: Fortress Press, 1994), 8.

4. J. Cheryl Exum and David Clines, *The New Literary Criticism and the Hebrew Bible* (Valley Forge, Pa.: Trinity Press International, 1993), 19.

5. David J. A. Clines, "Possibilities and Priorities of Biblical Interpretation in an International Setting," *Biblical Interpretation* 1 (1993), 78.

6. Randolph Tate, *Biblical Interpretation: An Integrated Approach* (Peabody, Mass.: Hendrickson, 1991), 148.

7. Ibid., xx.

8. Adele Berlin, "The Role of the Text in the Reading Process," *Semeia* 62 (1993), 144.

9. Peter Miscall, "Isaiah: New Heavens, New Earth, New Book," in *Reading between Texts: Intertextuality and the Hebrew Bible,* ed. D. N. Fewell (Literary Currents in Biblical Interpretation; Louisville: Westminster/John Knox, 1992), 45.

10. Stanley Hauerwas, *Unleashing the Scriptures: Freeing the Bible from Captivity to America* (Nashville: Abingdon, 1993).

11. Robert Robinson, "Wife and Sister through the Ages: Textual Determinacy and the History of Interpretation," *Semeia* 62 (1993), 104; Adele Berlin, "The Role of the Text," 143.

12. David Gunn, "New Directions in the Study of Biblical Hebrew Narrative," *JSOT* 50 (1987), 69.

13. Hauerwas, *Unleashing,* 36.

14. For example, Jack Miles, *God: A Biography* (New York: Knopf, 1995). See chapter 6.

15. The word "literal" is confusing in these discussions, because it can mean different things depending on the type of language and literature used. For example, I read the book of Jonah in basically a literal fashion, though it does not reflect something that actually happened. Narratively, Jonah *was* swallowed by a big fish.

16. David J. A. Clines, "Images of Yahweh: God in the Pentateuch," in *Studies in Old Testament Theology,* ed. David Hubbard et al. (Dallas: Word, 1992), 90.

17. See Terence Fretheim, *The Suffering of God: An Old Testament Perspective* (Overtures to Biblical Theology; Philadelphia: Fortress Press, 1984), 18-20.

18. See Terence Fretheim, "Genesis," *The New Interpreter's Bible,* vol. 1, (Nashville: Abingdon, 1994), for further discussion.

19. See Terence Fretheim, *Exodus* (Louisville: John Knox, 1991), for further discussion.

20. Elie Wiesel, *A Jew Today* (New York: Vintage, 1978), 6.

21. Kathryn P. Darr, "Ezekiel's Justification of God: Teaching Troubling Texts," *JSOT* 55 (1992), 117.

22. Timothy Beal, "The System and the Speaking Subject in the Hebrew Bible: Reading for Divine Abjection," *Biblical Interpretation* 2 (1994), 171. But cf. G. von Rad, *Old Testament Theology,* vol. 2 (San Francisco: Harper & Row, 1965), 415.

23. David Gunn and Danna Fewell, *Narrative in the Hebrew Bible* (Oxford: Oxford University Press, 1993), 28-29.

24. Danna Fewell and David Gunn, *Gender, Power and Promise: The Subject of the Bible's First Story* (Nashville: Abingdon, 1993), 22-38; James Barr, *The Garden of Eden and the Hope of Immortality* (Minneapolis: Fortress Press, 1992).

25. Philip Davies, "Abraham and Yahweh: A Case of Male Bonding," *Bible Review* 11 (1995), 25, 45.

26. Cf. Clines, "Images of Yahweh."

27. Walter Brueggemann, *Texts under Negotiation,* 72-75.

28. Gunn and Fewell, *Narrative,* 51.

29. Fewell and Gunn, *Gender, Power and Promise,* 18.

30. On metaphor, see T. Fretheim, *The Suffering of God,* 5-12, and the bibliography cited there.

31. For an analysis, see F. Watson, *Text, Church, and World: Biblical Interpretation in Theological Perspective* (Grand Rapids: Eerdmans, 1994), 19-29, 124-36.

32. For a study using these criteria, see Terence Fretheim, "The Repentance of God: A Key to Evaluating Old Testament God Talk," *Horizons in Biblical Theology* 10 (1988), 47-70.

33. For an earlier study of this matter, see my *Suffering of God,* and the bibliography there. For other texts, cf. Deut 7:6-11; Isa 30:28; 44:6; Jer 32:16-23; Neh 9:6-31; Pss 106; 136.

34. On the contingent nature of divine wrath, see A. Heschel, *The Prophets* (New York: Harper & Row, 1962), 279-98.

35. This is true across a wide theological spectrum. For recent efforts on the part of evangelicals, see Clark Pinnock et al., *The Openness of God: A Biblical Challenge to the Traditional Understanding of God* (DownerGrove, Ill.: InterVarsity, 1994).

36. See David Patte, *Ethics of Biblical Interpretation: A Reevaluation* (Louisville: Westminster/John Knox, 1995).

37. Gunn and Fewell, *Narrative,* 49.

38. Fretheim, *Deuteronomic History* (Nashville: Abingdon, 1983), 15.